MANAGING THE OBVIOUS

MANAGING THE OBVIOUS

HOW TO GET WHAT YOU WANT USING WHAT YOU KNOW

CHARLES A. COONRADT
with Jack M. Lyon and Richard L. Williams

Also by Charles A. Coonradt
The Game of Work
The Four Laws of Debt Free Prosperity

To my loving wife, Carla, and my children, Christina,
Kelly, Christopher, Cody, and Christian,
who have lived
through the experiences
that caused this book to be created,
and survived;
who taught me that the more we achieve,
the more the simple and basic principles
of family life mean.
Without you
none of this would have
been possible,
or very important.

The Game of Work, Inc.
1912 Sidewinder Drive, Suite 201
Park City, Utah 84060
e-mail cjc@gameofwork.com
800-438-6074

First edition, 1994
First printing March 1994
Second printing November 1996

Library of Congress Cataloging-in-Publication Data

93-080954

Coonradt, Charles A.
  Managing the obvious.

  Includes index.

ISBN 1-883004-01-2

Printed in the United States of America

10 9 8 7 6 5 4 3 2

Contents

14 Empowering Growth in Your Team   171
15 The Future Is Obvious   187

    Appendix   195
    Index   209

PREFACE

Why this book? I graduated in the '60s with a four-year degree, and I did it in four years. Then I still needed the advice and counsel of my dad, a high-school dropout who left school early to join the Navy in World War II. He later gained his GED through the service and graduated Magna Cum Laude from the school of hard knocks and bouncing back.

I later took courses in management and human relations skills; but it took a mentor, Paul J. Meyer to get me to set goals and learn of their motivational power for thousands. I took courses in speech, persuasion, and business letter writing; but it took the efforts of an ex-butcher from Minnesota, a coach from Tennessee, an ex-state highway engineer from Ohio, and a stockbroker from Michigan to teach me how to sell.

After the unimaginable success of *The Game of Work*, I became enthralled with the unending stream of concepts, ideas, and programs seemingly created by some unwritten code between the management consulting community and the managers of the world who are their customers. The list is endless: *Managing for Results, Up the Organization, Tough Minded Management, Leadership Effectiveness*, its companion *Parent Effectiveness Training, Transactional Analysis*, and on and on. They were filled with the secrets of position descriptions, assessment centers, performance appraisals, salary administration, and strategic planning—all the "new secrets" promising in just the course of reading a book or, at the most, attending a course lasting less than the equivalent of a twenty-four-hour day, you too could be transformed into the great manager or leader you always wanted to be.

We have searched for excellence, been taught what they didn't teach us at the Harvard Business School, learned to swim with the sharks, found our moment of truth, performed outrageous customer service, and even learned that for just a pair of dimes (oops, sorry Stephen, I meant a paradigm shift), we can practice the seven habits of highly effective people.

What is the appeal? Is it bound up in the human desire for improvement? Or is it a neurotic search for the lifeline by a group so insecure in their own devices that they are reaching for the illusion of correctness? Or is it, as I suspect, driven by the desire for the "quick fix"?

Most of the world's religions have existed for centuries. Their doctrines say the problem is not in finding a new way but following the old.

I have been intrigued by the popularity of Robert Fulghum and his neo Will Rogers observations of life, and by *Life's Little Instruction Books.* Their promise is not the new, quick-fix, insta-success but rather a rededication to the principles, not the platitudes, upon which real and lasting success has been and will continue to be based. This stuff is tough. Most of the success in life is. Simple, not easy, is the cornerstone of greatness and achievement. Join me and let's journey together through some familiar territory. Let us help you see things just a little differently.

So why this book? I wanted to simplify our search. I do not offer the ostrich approach of the U.S. Patent Office story in which a senator in the late 1800s suggested that the office be closed because everything of value had already been invented. You will not find "easy" contained herein. But life and managing (or coping) or parenting or mentoring never was, never is, and never will be easy. Instead, our mission is to make these things more simple, more straightforward, more fundamental, and, of course, more obvious.

A wise philosopher once said, "Procrastination is the fear of finding out what will happen if you act." I believe that is true. Eliminating procrastination is one of the cornerstone philosophies of Managing the Obvious. Let's take the first step together by getting into the basic concept.

ACKNOWLEDGMENTS

I want to thank my partner—that is my life partner, business partner, parenting partner, and eternal partner—my wife, Carla, without whom not only would this book not have been possible but my life would not have turned out the way it has.

I wish to thank and honor my parents, Helen and Ken. They showed me how to work, lived their lives dedicated to the simple and powerful truths that are timeless, and showed me that dedication and perseverance will take you where you want to go.

To my mentors, thanks, especially to Al Martindale, for without the sticking, needling, and constant reassurance this work would still be in the embryonic stage of good intentions. To Bob Raybould, who buoyed a sagging self-confidence and was always there to make me feel okay about a small measure of success. To William Shea, who took the time to show me what mentoring can mean.

Thanks for the examples of Paul J. Meyer, Rex Houze, Jim Sirbasku, and Ferrell Hunter, who taught me about goal setting, selling, and growth. They instilled self-belief in my own and others' unlimited potential.

Thank you to the thousands of chief executive officers and owners that have retained and used our concepts. These are people that hired us to teach and, in fact, wound up teaching me. Thanks to the hundreds of thousands of participants in our processes whose successful implementation of these concepts stands as their greatest proof.

Thanks to my co-authors. Lee Nelson, for his herculean effort in unmangling the manuscript of *The Game of Work* and creating a book that built our business. Thanks for the confidence of being able to call myself an author. To Jack Lyon for gutting through this maze and giving it structure, body, and organization. To Rick Williams for getting involved at the critical stage where we could have lost it all, picking us up, re-energizing this work, and "trail bossing" us to completion.

Is Success a Secret, or Is It Obvious?

An old management proverb says, "There's no such thing as all of a sudden." In most situations, there are warning signs like large flashing lights that tell us of impending problems. But it is our ability to see and accept these warning signs, and then our willingness to proactively make changes in our behavior, that enable us to prevent problems from turning into disasters.

- Have you ever seen a manager who procrastinated making a difficult decision, hoping the problem would resolve itself?
- Have you ever seen a manager literally ignore a problem with an employee because of a fear of confrontation?
- Have you ever heard about a person who experienced one of the seven cancer warning signs but did nothing about it until it was too late?
- Have you ever seen a parent who sees the warning signs that a child is on the wrong track but does nothing to help the child?

People believe that ignorance is bliss. But ignorance isn't bliss, it's just being ignorant!

Part of the problem stems from how many of us are

socially conditioned to ignore or even deny the obvious. Perhaps you were taught as a child, "If you can't say something good about someone, then don't say anything at all." Or, "If it ain't broken, don't fix it." Or, "Don't go where you're not wanted." Or, "Don't speak unless you are spoken to." Or, "Don't bother a sleeping dog." Or, "Respect your elders." Or, "Patience is a virtue."

More people fail because they are unwilling to deal with what they know than because they are the victims of some unforeseen fate. We have the ability, to a large extent, to control our successes and ultimate destiny with what we are willing to see, accept, and then act upon.

Many people throughout history have ignored the obvious. One of the more intriguing examples is the officers and crew of the luxury-liner *Titanic.*

DID THE OBVIOUS SINK THE TITANIC?

On the bitterly cold night of April 14, 1912, the *Titanic* was on her maiden voyage from Southhampton, England, to New York. The nearly 900-foot-long, eleven-story-high *Titanic* was the largest ship the world had ever known and was considered the consummate luxury liner of her day. She had double-bottom construction, and her hull was divided into sixteen watertight compartments. Because of her ultra-modern design and enormous size, she was considered unsinkable.

As she sliced through the icy waters of the North Atlantic at a swift twenty-one knots, not one of the more than 2,200 passengers and crew on board had any idea that the impending disaster would become a maritime legend. More than eighty years later, the sinking of the *Titanic* has become a symbol of a disaster that could have been prevented. It could have been prevented because the series of events that led up to the collision with an iceberg that night were obvious to the officers and crew.

WHAT OBVIOUS EVENTS PRECEDED THE COLLISION?

• The captain and crew of the *Titanic* knew they would reach an iceberg field about 9:30 P.M. that evening. Lookouts had been cautioned to be alert for icebergs, but the ship nonetheless plowed on at twenty-one knots on a dark, moonless night.

• The captain and crew had received at least seven warning messages over the radio from other ships that there were numerous icebergs in the immediate area. The danger to the *Titanic* was obvious, but the captain, crew, and even many of the passengers were confident of the ship's invulnerability. In fact, when the *Titanic* received a message from a nearby ship, the *Californian*, that it was stuck in an ice field only ten miles away, the *Titanic's* radio operator replied, "Shut up, shut up; keep out. I'm talking to Cape Race; you are jamming my signals."

• The sixteen lifeboats and four canvas collapsible boats were capable of accommodating only about 1,180 of the more than 2,200 passengers aboard the *Titanic*. The water temperature that night was 28 degrees. The crew knew, therefore, that in the event of a disaster more than a thousand people would die of hypothermia in a matter of minutes.

• Frederick Fleet, the lookout in the crow's-nest on the *Titanic*, wasn't given a pair of binoculars. Consequently, when he spotted the iceberg and rang a three-bell warning, it was already too late for Quartermaster Robert Hichens to avoid the collision.

• The *Californian's* radio operator, Cyril F. Evans, exhausted after a long day and angered by the *Titanic's* uncaring response to his warning about icebergs, went to bed about 11:30 P.M. and missed the *Titanic's* distress calls. Throughout that early morning, the *Californian* remained at rest only ten miles from the disaster site.

• The radio on the *Californian* was powered by a magnetic detector that had to be turned by hand. Charles Groves, the *Californian*'s third officer, didn't know this, so when he tried to listen to the radio after Frederick Fleet went to bed, he couldn't hear anything and gave up.

• During the four days, seventeen hours, and thirty minutes of the *Titanic*'s only voyage, there had been no boat drills to train the passengers and crew in the event of a disaster. The passengers didn't even have lifeboat assignments.

• Before the *Titanic* left port, one of the crew members was quoted as saying, "God himself could not sink this ship." Many crew members had a "ram-you-damn-you" attitude. They felt their purpose was to provide "express train" service across the Atlantic, even if it meant going full-tilt through ice fields.

WHAT WAS OBVIOUS AFTER THE COLLISION?

• After hearing the three-bell warning, Quartermaster Hichens gave the order "hard astarboard" and reversed the engines. Even so, the iceberg sliced a three-hundred-foot gash below the waterline. Within ten minutes the water was fourteen feet above the keel level.

• A full twenty-five minutes after the collision, Captain Smith ordered Chief Officer H.F. Wilde to uncover the lifeboats.

• After giving that order, Captain Smith walked about twenty yards down the port side of the boat deck to the wireless shack and said, "Send the call for assistance." But this order didn't happen until twenty minutes after he knew the fate of the *Titanic*.

• The *Californian*, with its radio operator in bed and radio turned off, was at a dead stop in the water only ten miles from the disaster site. The next closest rescue ship to hear the *Titanic*'s distress call was the *Carpathia*. At maximum speed, it took the *Carpathia* three and a half hours to reach the disaster site. The *Carpathia* missed the sinking of the *Titanic* by forty-five minutes. When she arrived, the *Titanic* was resting on the ocean floor, thirteen thousand feet below the surface. And more than a thousand people had already perished.

So Why Did She Sink?

Was it the obvious or the unknown that caused this tragedy? If the captain and crew had recognized the obvious facts of the situation, could they have prevented the disaster? Did the obvious or the non-obvious sink the *Titanic?* Maritime historians have debated these issues since 1912, but from a managerial perspective, it's obvious why the *Titanic* sank! The ship sank because White Star Lines (owner of the *Titanic*), Captain Smith, and many of the crew failed to manage the obvious.

Just like the crew of the *Titanic*, some modern managers fail to prevent disasters, reach their potential, and achieve success because they are unaware of, or sometimes even ignore, the obvious. The failure or inability of a manager to see or admit the obvious in today's business world can cause a tragedy not unlike that of the *Titanic*.

A Modern-Day Titanic?

The story and lesson of the *Titanic* continue to be repeated in the business world today. Consider, for example, the changes that happened to General Motors in the early 1990s, which created the greatest upheaval of a company that size in modern history. The question is, could GM's problems have been prevented? Were they obvious, or were they not? Many automobile industry analysts are convinced that GM's problems were obvious and could have been corrected before they created a crisis.

First, it's important to recognize how good the GM cars

were during the late 1980s and early 1990s. J.D. Powers and Associates ranked Cadillac and Buick among the industry's ten top makes for customer satisfaction during that time period. So product quality did not directly contribute to GM's problem. Also, GM was the industry leader in several critical technologies, such as antilock brakes and electric cars.

The severity of General Motors' problems was staggering. Prior to the announced cut-backs in the early 1990s, GM was 40 percent less productive than Ford. It was estimated that in 1991 GM lost on average $1,500 on every one of the more than 3.5 million cars and trucks it made in North America. In other words, GM lost $1 million an hour, twenty-four hours a day, seven days a week, for fifty-two weeks!

Just like the *Titanic*, General Motors received many warning messages of an impending disaster. For example, GM's market share eroded from 46 percent in 1979 to 35 percent in 1991. Ford and Chrysler also experienced problems, and both nearly went bankrupt in the early 1980s. This was an obvious signal of serious problems in the industry and should have been a portent of things to come for GM as well. From 1985 to 1992 GM's long-term debt more than doubled, and by 1992 it amounted to 35 percent of equity. In general, GM lagged behind its major competitors in almost every measure of efficiency.

All the obvious signals of an impending disaster were available. Still, GM's top officers essentially held on to the existing corporate structure and stifling policies that had created the problem. The chairman of the board/CEO preferred evolutionary, not revolutionary, solutions to the company's problems. He refused to consider combining his six-division marketing system to reduce costs and actually said that he would never reorganize the company. At that time an industry analyst said that the chairman's only chance of survival would be to make the company progress through change; he refused. It took GM's board of directors to convince him to make the 1991 and 1992 cut-backs and begin a reorganization of the company. After the changes were announced, an industry analyst said: "It looks like [the chairman] finally realizes the magnitude of the problems affecting the company."

The failure of GM's management team to accept and fix a series of small problems made it necessary for GM to face a staggering financial dilemma. An insider at GM said, "We did something [in 1992] that we should have done in the mid-eighties."

The captain of a cruise ship speeding ahead on a moonless night in the middle of an iceberg field is not much different from a company CEO who refuses to see the obvious warning signs of an impending financial disaster. In both cases it was easier for these people to reject undesirable facts than to accept those facts and take appropriate and corrective action. Even after the *Titanic* hit the iceberg, Captain Smith refused to believe that the ship could sink. Throughout the 1980s, the General Motors management team also refused to believe that their ship could sink. We know that the *Titanic* sank, but time will judge what will happen to General Motors after its collision with the obvious.

RECOGNIZING THE OBVIOUS

When you can recognize the obvious, you will improve your ability to act on the obvious events that shape your destiny. Never again will you need to ignore or deny the obvious. You don't have to let your ship or company sink.

- How can you improve your ability to see the obvious?
- How can you better manage the obvious?
- How can you help others see the obvious?

Why read this book? The answer is obvious!

WHAT'S OBVIOUS

Have you ever walked out of a meeting with a business associate and one minute later, back in your office, thought of what you *could* have said? Have you ever looked at the super-colossal regional shopping mall down the street and remembered when the property on which it stands was once selling for $400 an acre? Have you ever wished you had bought stock in Apple computers back when Steven Jobs was tinkering in his garage? If you have (and most of us have), then you've sensed what it means to discover the obvious—albeit a little bit late. But the purpose of this book is to help you discover the obvious things you need to do *now* to improve your odds for success. this book will help you do three things:

1. Avoid disaster.

2. Achieve improvement, excellence, or success in any area that is important to you.

3. Enjoy the journey of success, which is the journey between where you are now and where you want to go.

It will teach you to ask, seek, and knock, to open the door to opportunities that arise and will continue to arise as you pursue your goals. It will help you to look at your life with renewed vigor, vitality, and commitment. You are about to embark on one of the most stretching and potentially stressful journeys of your life—an adventure in adult learning. As you do so, you will learn three new sets of skills:

1. *Discovering the obvious.* This section will help you develop a skill that many great leaders have developed—a unique "vision," the ability to see what others cannot see or refuse to see. For example, in the 1970s, in the midst of the erosion of market share and profitability in the U.S. auto market, someone at Chrysler determined that there was an untapped market desire for the mini-van. And with that determination, Chrysler created a niche and established a leadership position that has withstood a decade of challenges.

You will learn the "why" and the "how" that gives the edge to successful managers, leaders, coaches, and parents. And maybe most important, you will learn how to discover the obvious *in advance.* Discovering the obvious is easy, after the fact. For example, today we can see many things that could have prevented the *Titanic* from sinking. But it's more difficult to identify the *Titanic*s in our own lives. In this book, we'll focus on how the discovery of the obvious can be the preventer of disaster and the predictor of success. We'll even dedicate a chapter to what you can do when the obvious *isn't* so obvious—show you how to crank up the microscope several more degrees. Just as scientists now believe they have confirmed the "Big Bang" theory, the depth of our investigation of the obvious is related to the power of our investigatory tool, and ours is powerful.

2. *Communicating the obvious.* Because none of us is an island, we all depend on the ability to communicate our ideas to those we look to for support, assistance, and shared achievement. Couples, business partners, managers and employees, parents and teenagers—all work in harmony or disharmony based on their ability to achieve and perpetuate consensus. "Well, that's obvious, Chuck," you are thinking—which means you're getting it already. But how we achieve that consensus and then, maybe even more important, keep it going is a real key to working as a team.

3. *Applying the obvious.* Many of the business books written today leave the reader thinking, "That's great, but how do I apply these principles?" or "Good ideas, but I

don't think they will work in our company." In this third section, we will give you specific examples and tools to help you apply the obvious in your business and in your life. Many clients have said that most of the "experts" in the world operate only from the neck up. I operate from the elbows down as well. Together, we will make these principles work.

The principles themselves are basic—obvious. You will find mastering them to be relatively easy. And once you begin using them, they will bring a harmony to your life and your work that most people only dream about. Our unique and obvious approach to teamwork will add years to your life, and, more important, a desire to live them.

THE LEARNING PROCESS

Many of us resist learning something new—sometimes with good reason. Remember what it was like learning to ride a bicycle? Remember the first day of swimming lessons? Real scary. And if I'm used to my trusty old IBM Selectric typewriter and somebody plants a word processor on my desk, I'll naturally be a little apprehensive. Will I be able to retrieve my files? What if the electricity goes off while I'm working? Does it emit harmful radiation? Will I ruin it if I hit the wrong key? If it's so much more efficient than a Selectric, will my co-worker soon be out of a job? Will I?

How we learn something new has been studied and debated by trainers, educators, psychologists, and instructional designers for years. One of the most interesting theories is from Tom Hopkins International of Scottsdale, Arizona, which says there are four levels of learning:

1. Unconscious incompetence.
2. Conscious incompetence.
3. Conscious competence.
4. Unconscious competence.

We progress from one through four in sequence whenever we learn something new.

1. *Unconscious incompetence.* This first stage is when we don't know what we don't know. Contrary to popular

opinion, ignorance is *not* bliss, and this is not usually a comfortable stage to be in. At this stage we may know something is wrong, but we just don't know what it is. (I believe this accounts for a great deal of the misery in life.) For example, a young child does not realize that shoes do not automatically come with a parent to tie them. So when the shoes come untied, she may spend quite a bit of time tripping over her laces before Mom or Dad comes to the rescue.

Similarly, many of us are a little too comfortable in our current management behavior to take advantage of opportunities that might be ours with a little investigation. But unlike the child, we don't have to continue tripping over our loose laces. We have the capacity and the tools, if we will use them, to figure out why we're falling down all the time. Unfortunately, our attitudes are too often hardened by years of rejection, embarrassment, and other "character building" experiences that prevent us from looking for or even admitting that new opportunities might exist. This resistance to change is highly debilitating because it cuts off learning before the possibility of change is even acknowledged. It is often manifested in the NIH (not invented here) mindset or in such idea-killing phrases as "We've always done it this way," "We've never done it that way," and "We already tried that ten years ago, and it didn't work." When you find this kind of ostrich-like, head-in-the-sand attitude blocking *any* new thinking, attack it with a vengeance. We all need encouragement to find out what we don't know.

The three best students of life I know, Paul J. Meyer, Jim Cosman, and Bernie Kenney, do not possess college degrees, but they have built their success by never failing to investigate an alternative. They taught me that we may not find the answer even if we look, but we are *assured* of not finding it if we don't.

2. *Conscious Incompetence.* At this stage we *know* that we don't know—a highly frustrating level. The child has now learned the shoes need to be tied, but she also realizes she can't tie them. What makes this stage difficult is that we were designed by our creator to keep striving for growth.

So the child keeps trying. In her frustration, she may pout, cry, and throw her shoes against the wall, but she does not give up. With every failure, she tries and tries again. Students of modern management technique will notice that the reaction of the average manager is not unlike that of the child, except for the willingness to try, try again. In fact, the manager who is well schooled and endowed with great natural talent and ability is often more likely to quit than the child. What a great testimony to the importance of attitude over aptitude in the struggle of life!

Another important factor at this stage is that Mom and Dad keep on coaching the child when she makes a mistake. "See, Susie? You make a loop on this side, and then you wrap the lace on this side around it. Try it again. You can do it." In business, too, we need to continually coach the members of our team, teaching them and encouraging them to succeed. We might think of this as the stage of excitement and discovery: "I wonder what we are going to learn from this?" At worst, we can accept it as a necessary evil in the establishment of a greater good.

It is important to realize that this stage is transitory—it does not last. Even the greatest student must have faith in his or her own ability to learn. When you can see progress, you find it easier to believe that you will ultimately succeed. Progress enhances the *desire to try,* which is so natural to children, and which many of us adults need some intellectual assistance to regain. You may choose to remain in this stage or to return to it periodically to ensure your continued improvement.

3. *Conscious competence.* This is the stage where we need reinforcement, the stage in which we need to look at the diagram of the Windsor knot that Land's End so conveniently places in their tie catalog. (Thank you, Land's End.) This is the stage in which we need to watch the review video before the annual diving trip to the Caribbean. This is where we know we can do a certain task or behavior, but we still feel the need to look at the directions and to pay close attention to what we are doing.

It's like the kid who has learned to ride a bicycle with

training wheels and doesn't actually *need* the training wheels anymore. But he or she would feel real uncomfortable if we took the training wheels off. At this stage, the kid needs continual reassurance and reinforcement. We need to keep saying, "Don't worry, we'll leave the training wheels on for now, but see how you don't really need them?" Those on our business team who reach this stage need similar encouragement and praise—possibly even more encouragement and praise than they really deserve.

We often feel inadequate at this stage, but without any good reason. We need to remember that it's okay and normal to look at the directions. Pilots, for example, keep us in the air by the use of a checklist. "Yes," you respond, "but I should be able to just manage naturally." Why should you? Everyone else goes through "learning curves," and the more complex their tasks, the more times they've had to do so. As in the previous stage, our greatest risk is in quitting. But we need to persist, even if we're a bit fearful or uncomfortable in our new-found skill. Great golfers, for example, were not born with a natural swing; quite to the contrary, it is their ability to adapt, change, and overcome bad habits that creates success for the majority of the top players. Look at the resurgence of players over forty years old who have employed the learning process with great success. You too can adopt those behaviors that will obviously add to your success. Check the checklist! Pilots do. (And thank goodness for that.) I sense no lack of pride in using a checklist to reinforce a desired attribute.

Joseph Albertson, for example, as he was building his supermarket empire, maintained a card on the likes and interests of his store-level employees. Then, before each store visit, he would review that information in order to make his business a more desirable place of employment. Was he being manipulative and insincere? Or did he simply find that the reinforcement checklist made him more effective? Using such lists is a way to maintain a behavior that we could easily do on a smaller scale but might find some trouble keeping up with as our business grows.

This is also the stage at which we respond best to the concept that Napoleon Hill, in his classic *Think and Grow Rich*, called "autosuggestion." Also described as affirmation, self-talk, and self-suggestion, autosuggestion is a way to program into the subconscious and conscious mind behaviors we want to reinforce. The mind needs this stage to make performance permanent and natural.

This stage must be viewed as a necessary step in acquiring any new behavior. Perhaps the leap of faith required, and reflected in the development of that desired quality of persistence, is the knowledge of how quickly this stage passes.

4. *Unconscious competence.* This is the stage of learning toward which we have been striving all along. A person who has reached this stage in a certain area is often described as a "natural," a "pro" who makes the difficult appear easy. When I am working with a group to help increase their productivity and profitability, I am often complemented on my "insight," my ability to penetrate to the heart of an issue. This is not a gift; it has just grown from experience with the many variations I have seen in company problems. It comes from the same process we see when an employee, after thirty years of tying a necktie or scarf before going to work, can do it with his or her eyes closed. Is this person a "natural" at tying the scarf or necktie? No, *he or she is just the natural product of the repeated application of a learned principle.* You can grow to that stage of competency in nearly any area with continuous practice.

THE POWER OF CHANGE

Whether you like it or not, learning and growth always mean change. Take a pencil and, on the lines below, list your reactions to the word *change:*

_____

_____

_____

_____

I always enjoy watching how people react to the word
change. As I ask people how they feel about that word, I
typically find a few who say, "Love it." But many more say,
"Afraid," "Concerned," "Apprehensive," and so on. I asked
one group that seemed particularly afraid of change, "Okay,
tell me one thing that never changes." They couldn't do it.
When you really think about it, there may be a few things,
like electricity at 110 volts in the United States. But nearly
everything around us is changing. So why is there so much
fear and apprehension?

Now review your reactions listed above. Are they
mostly positive, neutral, or a bit negative? It's important to
understand your attitudes toward change, because it's the
one thing in the world that is constant—which means
you're going to have to deal with it, whether you like it or
not. Let me introduce you to five concepts about change:

1. *Change is inevitable.* Dr. George Odiorne, the father
of management by objectives, said, "That which doesn't
change remains the same, and that which remains the same
quickly becomes obsolete." What things do you do or think
that are obsolete and need to change? Again pick up that
pencil and list them below (for example, 8088 computer
processors, leaded gasoline, typewriters). As your skill in
managing the obvious increases, return to the list to add
your discovered opportunities.

_____

_____

_____

_____

_____

_____

_____

One of the greatest skills we can practice is the acceleration of "the putting away of old things." Remember, even if you simply accelerate obsolescence, you are automatically becoming innovative!

2. *Change is constant.* Have you ever heard someone say, "The only thing that stays the same around here is the fact that they keep changing things"? Change is a force of life. Whether we consider the decline of the dinosaurs millions of years ago or the companies that went bankrupt yesterday, our lives are filled with the obvious principle of the constancy of change.

3. *Change can be either good or bad.* It depends to a large extent upon how much you understand about the change and the reasoning behind it, as well as the degree of change you have to undergo. Most of us have discovered the irony in the fact that whenever we have an idea for change, either at the office or around the house, it seems to be divinely inspired. However, my associates and family often seem to get their ideas for change from an entirely different source. And that brings us to the most important thing about change.

4. *All people view change egocentrically.* Most of us have an interesting attitude toward change. One side of us says, "Oh, good, something new!" The other side says, "Why can't things just stay the same?" But our attitude about change is usually controlled by how much we understand about the thing that's changing, and especially by how it will affect us personally. *Egocentric* is the most important word to keep in mind in managing change.

I'm excited about the changes in the now-defunct Soviet Union, for example, because I will have the continuing opportunity to go there and teach people about the Game of Work. I would love to help build the new Russian free-market economy. I also know somebody who lives there, so I can see how those changes will affect my friend. But the point is, I'm excited because I've decided those changes have a positive influence on my own life.

When Delta airlines bought PanAm, I didn't have very

many PanAm frequent-flier miles, so I thought, "Shoot, now all those PanAm people will be jumping on Delta planes—probably be harder to get a first-class upgrade." But the person with the PanAm miles thought, "Hah, lucked out on that deal!" And someone else was thinking, "Now I can go to Europe for less money." We all perceive such things individually, from our own perspective. So, when you want to control change in the future, think about how change influences motivation. What exchange values are being affected? Controlling change in the future means behaving in ways that will get the results you want with the values your team members have. Is that obvious? As you think about it, yes! Now you just need to decide what you're going to do with it.

People may appear to denigrate new ideas with the attitude of "What's in it for me?" But that attitude, in fact, is the *normal* response to change. When you show the exterior renderings of the proposed new office building to your team, notice the questions that come back:

Where is my office?

Where do I park?

What is the impact on my drive time?

Your initial response to their attitudes may be disgust, impatience, and some reflection on the character of the respondents. However, the benefit here is obvious: if we are bright enough to understand the integral aspect of those feelings, we can meet the needs of our organization by meeting the needs of the people within it. Now what are you doing with that obvious concept to improve the way you deal with change?

5. *We can choose how to deal with change.* We can choose to become the *changers,* or we can choose to remain the *changees.* Every day, we spend part of our lives achieving someone's goals; if we are not working on our own, then we must be working on someone else's. If we are not working on our personal goals of health and longevity, then we are supporting the goals of health-care providers and extended-care facilities. If we are not work-

ing on our goals of financial independence, then we are assisting those who lend money and profit from our unwise use of credit. If we are not working on our goals for improving the quality of our family life, then we are supporting the goals of the professionals who will be needed for intervention and remediation—perhaps for several generations.

Is this obvious? Yes, once you think about it. And that is what this book will help you do, so that down the road you won't be hitting yourself on the forehead and saying, "If only I had . . . " You've heard of the "Ah-hah!" experience? Looking back on the things we *wish* we had done is the "Ah, shoot!" experience: "If only I had . . . " "Why didn't I . . . " It's the kind of experience we want to avoid. This book will give you the concepts—and the tools—to define the obvious things you need to do now to achieve the success you desire.

DISCOVERING THE OBVIOUS

1

WHERE ARE YOU GOING?

few years ago, my friend Sue had some fairly serious health problems. She had been an invalid as a
child and still suffered from a birth defect that had
left a hole in one of the chambers of her heart. The
births of her five children, beginning with a difficult
C-section, had also taken their toll. She had suffered surgery
after surgery and had also put on weight for several years.
Diets had not helped her. She suffered almost constantly
from undiagnosed pain. Her husband, Dennis, had learned
to accept her limitations. He constantly hoped her health
would improve, but he did not really believe it ever would.

One day they sat down as a family and drew up a "wish
list" of the things they wanted most out of life. One of Sue's
items was to run in a marathon. Given her history and physical limitations, Dennis thought her goal was completely unrealistic, but Sue became committed to it.

She began by running very slowly in the subdivision
where they lived. Every day she ran just a little farther than
she had the day before—just one driveway more. "When
will I ever be able to run a mile?" Sue asked one day. Soon
she was running three. Then five. I'll let Dennis tell the rest
of the story in his own words:

> I remember Sue telling me something she had
> learned: "The subconscious and the nervous system

cannot tell the difference between real and vividly imagined situations." We can change ourselves for the better and cause ourselves to subconsciously pursue our most precious desires with almost total success if we crystalize the images clearly enough in our minds. I knew Sue believed it—she had registered to run in the St. George marathon in southern Utah.

"Can the mind believe an image that will lead to self-destruction?" I asked myself as I drove the mountainous road from Cedar City to St. George. I parked our van near the finish line and waited for Sue to come in. The rain was steady, and the wind was cold. The marathon had started over five hours ago. Several cold and injured runners had been transported past me, and I began to panic. The image of Sue alone and cold, off the road somewhere, made me sick with worry. The fast and strong competitors had finished long ago, and runners were becoming more and more sparse. Now I could not see anyone in either direction.

Almost all of the cars along the marathon route had left, and some normal traffic was beginning. I was able to drive directly up the race route. There were still no runners in view after driving almost two miles. Then I went around a bend in the road and spotted a small group running up ahead. As I approached, I could see Sue in the company of three others. They were smiling and talking as they ran. They were on the opposite side of the road as I pulled off and called between the now-steady traffic, "Are you okay?"

"Oh, yes!" Sue said, panting only mildly. Her new friends smiled at me.

"How far to the finish line?" one of them asked.

"Only a couple of miles," I said.

A couple of miles? I thought. *Am I crazy?* I noticed that two of the runners were limping. I could hear their feet sloshing in wet sneakers. I wanted to say to them that they had run a good race and offer them a ride in, but I could see the resolve in their eyes. I turned the van around and followed from a distance, watching for one or all of them to fall. They had been running for over five and a half hours! I sped around them and up to within a mile of the finish and waited.

As Sue came into view again, I could see her begin to struggle. Her pace slowed and she grimaced. She looked at her legs in horror as if they did not want to work any longer. Somehow, she kept moving, almost staggering.

The small group was becoming more spread out. Only a woman in her twenties was near Sue. It was obvious that they had become friends during the race. I was caught up in the scene and began running along with them. After a hundred yards or so I tried to speak, to offer some great words of wisdom and motivation, but my words and my breath failed.

The finish line came into sight. I was grateful it had not been completely dismantled, because I felt that the real winners were just now coming in. One of the runners, a slim teenager, stopped running, sat down, and started to cry. I watched as some people, probably his family, came and carried him to their car. I could also see that Sue was in agony—but she had dreamed about this day for two years and she would not be denied. She knew she would finish, and this knowledge allowed her to confidently—even happily—pick up her pace the last hundred yards to the finish line.

Few people were left to congratulate my wife and marathon runner extraordinaire. She had run a smart race, stopping to stretch regularly, drinking plenty of water at the various water stops, and pacing herself well. She had been the leader of a small group of less-experienced runners. She had inspired and encouraged most of them home with her words of confidence and assurance. They openly praised and embraced her as we rejoiced in the park.

"She made us believe we could do it," her new friend stated.

"She described how it would be to finish so vividly that I knew I could do it," another said.

The rain had quit, and we walked and talked in the park. I looked at Sue. She was carrying herself differently. Her head was more erect. Her shoulders were squared. Her walk, even though she was limping, had a new confidence. Her voice held a new, quiet dignity. It was not as if she had become someone new; it was more as if she had discovered a real self she had not known before. The painting was not yet dry, but I knew she was an undiscovered masterpiece with a million things left to learn about herself. She truly liked her newly discovered self. So did I. (Used by permission.)

DEFINING SUCCESS

Was my friend Sue a success? I suppose that depends on how you define success. She didn't make a million dollars. She didn't become the CEO of a major corporation. But I have no reservations in saying that she was definitely a success.

How do you define success? Napoleon Hill defines it as the continuous pursuit of a worthy ideal. Paul J. Meyer, founder of Success Motivation Institute, says that success is the progressive realization of worthwhile, predetermined personal goals. Christopher Morley wrote, "There is only one success—to be able to spend your life in your own way."

Ask several of your acquaintances if they would like to be more successful, and their response will usually be almost automatic: "Yes! Of course!" But now make that question a little more specific: "What does success mean to you?" Their intensity and response will probably dwindle into silence. Then they may offer a few definitions: money, happiness, contentment with their possessions, self-satisfaction, health, wisdom, freedom from strife and adversity. What great concepts, what sweeping generalities! But where lies the real meaning? How will they know when they've achieved it?

An example of someone who was willing to carefully define what he wanted out of life is well-known adventurer John Goddard. In his teens, he made a list of 127 things he wanted to accomplish. The list included such diverse items as traveling to the moon, becoming an Eagle Scout, flying every kind of airplane, learning shorthand, finding the heads of the world's major rivers, serving a mission for his church, and holding his breath underwater for two minutes. Now, decades later, as a sort of real-life Indiana Jones, he has completed more than a hundred of these goals. Has Goddard been successful? He certainly thinks so.

Lou Holtz, now head football coach at Notre Dame, had a rough childhood. He grew up in a poor family along the Ohio River where Ohio, West Virginia, and Pennsylvania converge, among the potteries and steel mills. He was able to escape a life sentence working in the mills by attending Kent State, where he played as a little-noticed linebacker. After graduation, he became an assistant coach at various schools. Finally, when his position was eliminated at the University of South Carolina, he had had enough. He made a list of 107 goals, with such items as landing on an aircraft carrier and being named Coach of the Year. The list also included, naturally enough, leading his favorite team, the Fighting Irish. Nineteen years later, in 1985, that particular dream came true, and under his direction the team's performance has been phenomenal. "When you sit down and set goals like this, you don't do it to impress other people," Holtz says. "You don't decide to do something so you can say, 'I did it, and you didn't.' You do it because you want to do it. . . . I want to make a hole in one, see the Pope, go to the White House for dinner, . . . see all my children graduate from college, float down the Snake River, jump out of an airplane. . . . I'd like to do that soon." (*Saturday Evening Post*, September 1989, p. 104.) Holtz's thirty-five-minute motivational video has sold briskly, and the coach is booked up on the lecture circuit at over $10,000 per appearance. He has his own syndicated cable TV show and a national radio call-in program. And he continues to lead Notre Dame to victory. How long can his success go on? "I don't think we can win every game," he says carefully. "Just the next one." (*Time*, November 27, 1989, p. 92.)

It all comes from knowing what you want. Henry David Thoreau offered this advice: "If one advances confidently in the direction of his dreams, and endeavors to live the life which he has imagined, he will meet with a success unexpected in common hours." And Benjamin Disraeli said, "The secret of success is constancy to purpose."

What are your dreams? What is your purpose? What do you want from life? If the answer to these questions is not immediately obvious to you, why not take out a sheet of paper and make out your own wish list before going on to the next chapter? List all your goals—all the things you would like to have, all the things you would like to do, all the things you would like to be, all the things you would like to have happen in your life. As you do this, don't think about limitations, judgments, or criticisms. Just write down the things you would most like to see become reality. Deciding on and listing these things may be the most important thing you ever do.

Have you heard this before? What have you done about it? If the answer is "nothing," then obviously *now* is the time to write down those goals. What prevents you from doing so? Don't have a pen? Buy a BIC. Ask a friend. *Just do it.* This is the simplest, most obvious of all that is obvious. If you won't do this, you may find the rest of the book a bit uncomfortable. If you will, who knows what wonderful things might happen?

Success comes not only to the mighty; it comes to any of us who set a goal, however small, and work to achieve it. As Russell Conwell said in his classic *Acres of Diamonds*, "If you wish to be great at all, you must begin where you are and with what you are. . . . He who can be a good citizen . . . , he who can make better homes, he who can be a blessing whether he works in the shop or sits behind the counter or keeps house, whatever be his life, he who would be great anywhere must first be great in his own [home town]."

2

WHERE ARE YOU NOW?

In 1991, a friend of mine, Stan, was having trouble with his fifteen-year-old son, Gary (not their real names). Gary's grades at school, not good before, had sunk to an all-time low of straight F's. Gary was having trouble at home, too. He often fought with other members of the family, especially his mother, and Stan was constantly stepping in to smooth things over. It wasn't long before Gary was threatening to run away. Stan and his wife, Nancy, had just about given up hope when the final blow came: a teacher called to say that Gary was using drugs.

Stan and Nancy called a drug rehabilitation clinic that night and confronted Gary the next morning. To their surprise, he agreed to go to the clinic. He wouldn't have to stay, he said, because he "didn't have a problem." In the first few minutes with the drug counselor, Gary denied everything. Ten minutes later, after a group of kids already in the program had nailed him to the wall, he admitted to using everything from marijuana to cocaine. Two weeks later, in a meeting with the other kids and families, Gary stood with tears running down his cheeks. "I've been using drugs for three years," he said, "and I don't know how to stop. I guess I really do have a problem. I'm an addict."

That was a turning point in Gary's treatment. When he could see himself as he really was, he could stop blaming other people for his problems, and things began to get better. But Gary wasn't the only one who had to change. Every member of the family needed to take a close look at themselves. As Stan later told me, "Because I was always stepping in to smooth things over for Gary, he never had to face the fact that he had a problem. And I never had to face the fact that I had one too. Now our family is fairly sane again. But for me, sanity is finding out what I don't like about myself."

THE POWER OF NEGATIVE THINKING

In the previous chapter, we talked about the need to know where we want to go. But equally important is the need to see clearly where we are now. If we don't know where we are now, we will never know how to get to where we want to be. Most of us, like Gary and Stan, have a hard time being objective about where we really are. The reasons are many, but I believe the most prevalent is an *unwillingness* to admit into consciousness the current state of affairs. Business writer Robert J. Ringer explains the problem this way: "Human beings have a tendency to wave aside the obvious. Intellectually, we may agree with a point that's apparent, but when it comes time to act, we often ignore our intellect and act on emotion. . . . The fact is that most people live in a totally *unreal* world. They create a world in their own minds based on the way they would *like* the world to be rather than the way it actually *is*. All of us, to one extent or another, have adopted the philosophy of the popular humorist Ashleigh Brilliant, who once remarked, 'I have abandoned the search for truth, and am now looking for a good fantasy.' . . . It is absolutely essential that a person intellectually and emotionally understand that reality isn't the way he wishes things to be or the way they appear to be, but the way they actually *are*. The person who is not able to make this distinction finds it virtually impossible to make decisions that lead to positive results." (*Million Dollar Habits* [New York: Wynwood Press, 1990], pp. 13-14.)

I believe we see the truth of this statement every day—

most often in our own lives. For example, most people who are overweight inaccurately assess their eating habits and current weight or body fat content. Similarly, when the bloom goes out of a relationship, few of us have the integrity to admit what portion of the problem is ours.

I asked one party in a dissolving marriage, "What would *you* have to do differently to make this thing work?" In response, he gave me the blankest stare I have ever seen. Then he began to reply, "Well, she would have to—" I cut him off, asking him to answer my original question. He returned to the blank look, and I could practically read his mind. He was thinking, "Who, me? Why, I've never even thought about that."

As the first step to recovery from alcoholism, Alcoholics Anonymous requires a person to make an affirmation like this one: "My name is Ken, and I am an alcoholic." That is a powerful example of recognizing the current situation as the first step in making progress.

I know a golfer, a twenty-two handicapper, who simply cannot understand when any shot goes wrong. He would do better to be surprised when a shot goes right. But he hasn't accurately assessed his true status as a golfer.

There is great power in periodically reexamining our assumptions—in seeing which ones no longer work and which ones have made it impossible for us to grow and achieve. Take some time to figure out where you are in various areas of your life. Ask yourself, "How long have I been on this plateau? Have I given in to a certain comfort level, and is my present attitude sacrificing my future commitment to progress?"

If you are overweight, for example, figure out how much weight you have gained in the past year. Ten pounds? What if you gain that much again this year? And next year? And unless you change the pattern, doesn't that mean that five years from now you'll be more than *fifty* pounds heavier than you should be? It's an obvious conclusion, but how many of us are willing to face up to it?

It's like the executive whose gross profit margin is so

dangerously low that the business may have to be sold. We ask, "How long have you known there was a problem?"

"Well, I knew three years ago that overhead expenses were growing too fast."

"Have you done anything about it?"

"Well, not really. I've had too many other things to think about."

Or, on a more personal note, how long has it been since your spouse said he or she loved you? And what do you think that means?

"KNOW THYSELF"

Why not take a minute to find out where you are right now? Let's start with your physical attributes.

	KNOW	CAN FIND OUT	CANNOT FIND OUT
Height	___	___	___
Weight	___	___	___
Age	___	___	___
Heart rate	___	___	___
Blood pressure	___	___	___
Respiratory rate	___	___	___
Cholesterol level	___	___	___
Blood sugar level	___	___	___
Exercise heart rate	___	___	___

Can you determine each of these attributes? Of course. And for each of these obvious physical traits, you can determine an appropriate response.

You are probably saying, "Well, that's easy." That's exactly the point. We want to start with the easy and obvious things in your life that need attention and then move progressively toward recognizing the things that may not be so obvious. Now let's expand a bit. Let's look at the financial aspect of your life.

	Know	**Can Find Out**	**Cannot Find Out**
Last year's salary	___	___	___
Last year's expenses	___	___	___
Personal net worth	___	___	___
Desired income at retirement	___	___	___
Home mortgage balance	___	___	___
Mortgage payoff date	___	___	___
What year each of your children will start college	___	___	___
Tuition for each child	___	___	___
When you will buy your next vehicle	___	___	___
Cost of your next vacation	___	___	___

As you can see, answering questions like these is not particularly difficult. But knowing the answers can make a great difference in how you run your life.

If you're going to get serious about managing the obvious, you'll need a set of questions, like those above, that are designed especially for you. Take a minute right now to write down some of the obvious questions about your life. When you have exhausted your own ideas, ask your spouse for help. Ask a business associate to help you list questions about the obvious areas in your company. Ask a friend to help you identify the obvious questions in a non-financial area of your life, such as a church assignment, a civic project, or even the neighborhood cleanup or crime-watch program. Ask your doctor about your health.

In this, as in all other areas of life, practice does not make perfect; practice makes permanent. Only perfect practice makes perfect. But in the pursuit of the obvious, we need to develop the selective perception that comes from identifying the easy questions and then, with that perception, move to the questions that are harder to recognize.

To do this, take that first set of questions and add more questions that are *suggested* by the first ones. Next, prioritize the entire list. Finally, cross out those that are insignificant. In this exercise, as in the one in the preceding chapter, avoid limitations, judgments, and criticisms; creativity precedes criticism, here as well as in the dictionary.

I have had experience with many retail operations that have an especially hard time recognizing their own invalid perceptions and preconceived ideas. They aren't stupid. It's just that the way they do things is "the way it's always been done." Many retailers, for example, spend amounts equal to their net operating profits to attract price-sensitive customers in the hope that one visit will turn those customers into loyal shoppers—even when they know they cannot afford to have those price-sensitive shoppers continue to buy only the promotional items. They also know that those marginal shoppers disappear the moment the promotional pricing program disappears. Don't they? Sometimes I wonder. A multi-store furniture retailer spent $600,000 in advertising each year to attract 40,000 shoppers. (I checked.) That is a per-shopper attraction cost of approximately $15.00. But with a sales-closing ratio of 33 percent, it's really $45.00 to attract one purchasing customer. When you factor in the average purchase of over $1,100, the attraction cost fits within a less-than-5-percent guideline affordable in that industry. Why that is a criterion for success is beyond me, but it is the basis for some incredible logic.

Anyway, this is just another story until you check the company's future strategy. How do you satisfy your best customers and then find more just like them? How much would you spend on asking your *current* buyers to *return?* (Before you answer, remember that it cost $45.00 to attract a new buyer, one we know nothing about—unlike our previous buyers, for whom we know home style, home size, credit-worthiness, family size, and many other things, because of information we asked for on the credit applications for their major purchases.) How much would you spend? How much did they? Fifty cents apiece. That's right, fifty cents. They traditionally sent their customers one thank-you card thirty days after their purchase and never contacted them again with anything other than the general media offerings. Is it any wonder that this company, two decades old, did not make it into the nineties?

Continuing to do things in the same old way is like driving a car at night. We may know exactly where we want to go, but unless we turn on the headlights so we can see where we are, we're more likely to drive into a ditch than to reach our destination. And we need to keep those headlights on, periodically reviewing our progress toward the place we want to go.

3

What to Do When the Obvious Isn't

At times, what should be obvious just isn't obvious at all—at least not until later when it hits us right in the face. *Then* it becomes obvious real fast. That's one reason professional athletes spend so much time watching videos of their performance. They're trying to see the mistakes that are not so obvious while they are playing but that quickly become obvious upon later review.

Similarly, "charting" has been widely used by athletes to discover patterns in their own play and in the play of their opponents—patterns that are not readily apparent to the unaided eye. What are these athletes looking for—absolutes? No, just tendencies. For example, they want to know what their opponents will be *likely* to do under a particular set of circumstances—not so they can have complete control of the situation, but so they can profit from the probabilities of the situation. If I can expect a certain behavior from my opponent, or from the marketplace, or from a prospect, or from myself, for that matter, then I can use that knowledge to increase my chances for victory.

When we have a problem in business, we can't ordinarily videotape our performance to find out what we're doing wrong. But one thing we can do is to *dig*, to find the facts that lie at the bottom of the problem. Like most successful research, this digging is best approached through commitment to a set of research principles. The most critical of these is the biblical admonition to ask, seek, and knock. We must be as willing to examine our past behavior, experimentally, as we would to examine the behavior of laboratory animals or the weather patterns from which we formulate tomorrow's forecast.

For some reason, most of us are not willing to make that kind of objective self-examination. Seeing the faults and foibles of someone *else*, on the other hand, is much easier, and one of the things my associates and I enjoy doing is analyzing the business patterns of our clients to help them discover the not-so-obvious causes of their sometimes highly obvious problems.

Over the years, we have learned that we cannot usually solve a problem where it manifests itself. Instead, we must go back to where the problem begins. In a metals manufacturing company I worked with, for example, the problem manifested itself when the company did not have enough cash—a common but serious problem. *What happened just before we saw the problem?* Not enough money was paid on the outstanding receivables. We asked the obvious question: Were the collectors doing their job correctly? In this case, yes. We saw a day or two more than we should have in "days of sales uncollected," but that did not explain the entire problem. In fact, we saw that even if we got herculean efforts from collections, we could not solve the cash crunch.

What happened just before we saw the problem? Not enough accounts receivable were due to be collected.

What happened just before we saw the problem? Not enough sales were being invoiced. Were there sales that had been produced or delivered but not invoiced? We checked the records and learned something very interesting: the sales reps were immensely successful in getting customers to accept billing on custom items that would be delivered during the subsequent month. Mortgaging the future is not usually wise, but this was not really the source of the problem either.

What happened just before we saw the problem? Not

enough production had been generated to be invoiced. Were there orders that could be produced that were not yet being done? We checked the records and learned that there were not. The production department was manufacturing everything that was scheduled, and in fact some extra labor hours appeared to be available if the work was there to be done.

What happened just before we saw the problem? Was there a backlog of work that needed to be scheduled? No. The company was even doing some work ahead of schedule to keep the production department busy and to avoid layoffs.

What happened just before we saw the problem? Not enough sales were being made to build the backlog. We had reached the head of the cash stream only to learn that the new business coming into the system was not a cascade but a trickle. Intriguingly enough, this fine, fifteen-year-old company had never tracked, reinforced, or expected performance at this level directly. They knew, of course, that this was an important area, but they thought that if they worked hard, and the economy was perking along, and their competitors didn't need the business too badly, and their customers would remember them when they needed something, then everything would be all right. That is not a very proactive way to run a business; it makes us feel that we are the victims of our destiny rather than its creators. But that *still* wasn't the answer to the problem.

So again we asked, *What happened just before we saw the problem?* We didn't know how much of the work being bid was being accepted by the customers. Without that information, we couldn't know how much more effort was required, and of course we couldn't know if the problem was based on the quantity or quality of the company's efforts. It's tough to make a decision or find a solution when we haven't done the correct diagnostics work.

So we started digging again. Were there any records of the facts we needed to do the diagnosis? As a matter of fact, we knew the number of sales booked, which was a great stroke of luck. Unfortunately, though, we had no history on the amount of bids submitted, their size, or why they were accepted or rejected. Should we have quit? No. We just needed to start tracking the necessary information from that point on. It would not be accurate for a while—today's results were in part due to the efforts of the team over the previous days, weeks, and months. But it was a starting point, and that was what we needed to make the beginning of the search for the obvious.

Armed with this new information, the sales manager and the general manager began to establish realistic targets for the increased bidding level required to gain the necessary booking levels of business, and the company achieved an increase in sales of over 25 percent in less than nine months! The profit improved from slightly above break-even to double-digit return on investment and provided the cash flow for moving the business to the next generation while providing the founder with an appropriate retirement package.

The important question at each step along the way was, as you will recall, *"What happened just before we saw the problem?"* By asking yourself that question, you can uncover all sorts of wonderful information about your business.

Notice too that at each step we could improve performance, even though we had not yet uncovered the ultimate cause of the problem. We could also design and leave in place a scorecard at each level to ensure continued effectiveness. However, the real prize lay in finding the source of the problem.

GETTING AN OUTSIDE POINT OF VIEW

Another way to obtain new insights into your business is to get an outside point of view—ask other people to tell you the things that look obvious to them. There are four kinds of people who can best do that:

1. Customers—the traditional kind from outside your business, as well as "internal customers" such as managers

of other departments. Pay special attention to those you find a little difficult to get along with; they are apt to be particularly candid about how you can improve.

2. Suppliers. Although suppliers are not traditionally on the list of people we have to satisfy, they probably see the business quite clearly and may have valuable insights that can contribute to your success.

3. Competitors. Although I am against focusing on what the competition is doing rather than on what *we* should be doing, I must admit that competitors can be valuable sources of feedback and information. Find a way to stay in touch.

4. Peers, neighbors, and friends. Too many of us are unwilling to ask those around us for a candid analysis of our business. In many progressive accounting and law practices, firms visit each other's offices for formal "practice analysis" and peer review. The National Automobile Dealers of America have a full-time staff dedicated to maintaining "Twenty Groups" made up of similar sized dealers from noncompetitive areas who share statistics, ideas, and, again, peer review. Many retailers in the grocery industry have followed suit with "share groups." In San Diego, for example, the Executive Committee provides a structured way for executives to meet and review each other's goals, dreams, and, yes, even excuses under the watchful eye of the most critical audience in the world—people just like themselves. Find your national or local equivalent and join up.

Of course, you don't necessarily need the formality of an outside service. Many years ago, Napoleon Hill, in his classic *Think and Grow Rich*, discussed the concept of the "mastermind group." Find six associates, people with interests similar (but not identical) to yours, and establish a mutual benefits agreement and a schedule for visiting each other's facilities and reviewing each other's statistics. A group of six provides two monthly visits a year, which is just often enough to provide valuable insight without taking too much time. (We will be happy to send you a suggested outline for conducting these sessions.)

TAKING THE CUSTOMER'S POINT OF VIEW

Sometimes what seems to be so complicated can be reduced to the obvious with several simple questions. One of the best ones is a spin-off from the Golden Rule: How would I like to be treated if I were the one being served by my organization?

A pediatric dentist in southern California has been able to build a very large practice because he asked himself this question and decided to look at his business literally as his clients did. He got down on his knees and crawled through the office one day, keeping his eyes at the same level as those of the average three-year-old. This gave him a definite understanding about how he could make his office a more pleasant place for children, and he made the changes necessary to bring that about. What changes? Well, kid-sized chairs in the waiting room, for example. Kid-level handles on the restroom doors. And, perhaps most important, fuzzy stuffed animals to hold while waiting to see the man with the drill. Once you see things as your customers see them, what you have to do to serve them more effectively becomes very obvious.

Another example is Dr. Folkman, a general practitioner whose practice started out at $280,000 per year with about $90,000 taken out for personal income—not enough; like so many professionals, the good doctor had no business school experience and had financed his education with the money lenders, racking up nearly a third of a million in debt before he ever saw his first dollar of revenue. Now he needed to know how to build his practice and keep his professional stature without becoming involved in marketing. His practice was made up of about two thousand patient visits each year, with revenue per patient of $140 a visit.

"Are you doing all you can for your existing patients?" I asked.

"Of course," he replied. "When they're sick, they come to see me, and I treat them."

"That's great," I said. "But do they all have the capacity to know when they need to be here? Do any of them ever come in too late to be treated? Could earlier diagnosis ever prevent anguish, pain, or even death?"

Dr. Folkman, conscientious physician that he was, immediately understood my point, and we began to explore the ways he could increase his service to his patients. Annual physicals would help anticipate problems, increase patient awareness, and meet the doctor's deeply felt goals of extending life and improving the quality of that life. But how could we get people to come in regularly once a year? Well, when do people think about how they are feeling? On their birthdays, of course. Counting the doctor's files, we discovered that he had more than forty-five hundred patients, and every one of them had a birthday! What could we do to celebrate? Give them a gift! The doctor created an offer of a free test, easy for the staff to administer and valuable in raising his patients' awareness of their need to maintain good health. The plan worked! Most of the people who received the card called to schedule an appointment. Some had to be called and reminded, but even those who did not schedule an appointment expressed appreciation for being remembered, and they asked for a follow-up call or promised to call the doctor in the future. And obviously they would. Not only did the doctor achieve his goal of providing quality health care for his patients, but in less than four years his practice approached $1 million in annual gross revenues, with more than four thousand patient visits and an average fee per visit of $240—significant increases in the humanitarian as well as the financial aspects of his business.

Many of us have not given the best service we are capable of giving, simply because we have not reached out to our customers. Think about the professionals who fill your needs: personal grooming, home maintenance, auto repair and maintenance, and even memberships in cherished organizations. How many times would your expenses have been reduced or your enjoyment enhanced if you had received a phone call or a written reminder of the opportunity to take timely action? Ever had to have your disc brakes resurfaced or replaced because the maintenance was not timely? Ever looked shaggy for that important business meeting because you forgot to make an appointment at the salon? There are many things we can do to better serve our customers—not just to increase our business but to better meet their needs, increase their satisfaction, and deserve their loyalty.

TURNING THE OBVIOUS PROBLEM INTO THE OBVIOUS SOLUTION

One hot summer, we were invited to help improve managerial performance for a major regional food retailer. We had been successful in improving sales and profits in another division and were invited into this group of stores to counteract the tremendous loss resulting from the difference between the gross-margin dollars that should have come from the pricing policy and the actual gross dollars calculated after the actual inventory was taken, purchases were accounted for, and an actual gross margin was determined. How much, you say, could you lose? Well, on an anticipated gross margin of 34 percent, the total gross margin percentage was coming out at less than 22 percent, a shrink of over $5 million dollars per year. (*Shrink* is a euphemism for the stuff we throw away, break, lose, or have stolen.) The division president was real concerned (an enormous understatement) and wanted to find and destroy the culprit.

Our second session concentrated on a group problem-solving session centered around the question "What do we believe the cause to be?" The ideas came quickly: We are too far from the source of supply; our checkers don't do the proper coding job; we have poor rotation on the part of our nonmanagement personnel; we use poor ordering practices; the supplier (outside of the company ownership) doesn't care about quality; and on and on they came. This kind of exercise works best when allowed to run its full course, until every last one of the possibilities has been thought of and listed. It is important not to criticize or be at all judgmental in making the list, which can be cleaned up and pared down later. The object of the session is to get as many ideas as possible, no matter how unlikely they are. There were exactly fifty items on the list when the imagination of the group was exhausted.

"Anything else?" I asked. No one spoke. "Good," I said. "Then let's list the ideas in descending order of priority and correctability. Each of you pick what you think are the ten most important elements to solve, then assign a point value of 10 to the most important, 9 points to the second most important, 8 points to the third, and so on, until your list is ranked in descending order of importance. Our staff will then calculate the master priority, and we can address the most important (and *obvious*) change required."

I must mention that the group was made up of store managers, produce department managers, and the division merchandising staff. Without exception, the top vote-getters were the things the managers could control the least. But that might have been expected; nearly all of us lay the blame for our problems on outside circumstances from time to time. This group blamed checkers, baggers, stockers, and, incredibly enough, even the customers, who were "fickle in their selection process"—they didn't buy in exactly the way the stores were putting out the merchandise. The president and I were disappointed but not surprised. How could we get these good folks to be more insightful about their situation?

A little probing was in order. "Are all the stores' problems of a similar size?" I asked. The answer was no, so we drew an asymptotic curve (see the appendix for information on creating an asymptotic curve) for the entire fifty-four stores and found that the shrink problems ranged from a low of 5.5 percent (quite acceptable) to an atrocious level of almost 18 percent (more than half of the expected gross margin). We asked the people to recall what it was about the better-performing stores that was different from the others. Better sales? That, of course, is the cure—or should we say mask—for so many problems. Yes, there was some indication that volume was a determining factor, but not reliably enough to produce a complete conclusion. There seemed to be something else.

Because we knew some of the shrink must be coming from what was being thrown away and not sold, I asked, "What about inventory levels? How many days of inventory do you have on hand in each store? The vice-president of produce spoke right up: "Only about eight days," he declared with obvious pride. The president and I were flabbergasted. Eight days was at least 50 percent more inventory than this company had determined was acceptable and appropriate. According to guidelines available in most trade publications, very efficient produce departments can operate on four days of merchandise, and even mediocre ones can do it with five or six days of merchandise on hand. When the inventory gets beyond that length of time, not only does freshness suffer and customer satisfaction become harder to maintain, but invariably more merchandise spoils and must be marked down (sold at less than a full profit margin) or thrown away (at a total loss). This also involves more labor and other expense. The obvious solution is to have what we need to sell when we need to sell it, and then to *sell* it.

To make the point more graphic, we asked the vice-president of produce to compare an asymptote of the shrink to an asymptote of the inventory on hand. It was almost a perfect mirror. In other words, where inventory was the heaviest, the shrink or loss factor was the greatest.

"That's obvious," you are probably saying, and if you are, you are getting the message. This is again an example of dealing with the facts and information at hand and not looking to the outside for the problems. But even with this overwhelming evidence of a problem/solution (and I have joined these two words because I believe that within every problem is a solution, which, when implemented, brings even greater benefits than simply solving the problem)— even with this overwhelming evidence, we faced a lack of acceptance on the part of the vice-president of produce. After all, we were asking him to change his style and his department, and, in an indirect way, to admit that his previous approach was wrong.

We seem to have an attitude, perhaps developed from the Judeo-Christian ethic, that in order to adopt a new attitude or behavior, we must repent—that is, admit that what we have been doing all along has been wrong. Our search for the obvious is further hindered by that little voice of self-blame we all possess that says, "Dummy, you should have thought of that before!" Please resist this trap. Our techniques for discovering what ought to have been obvious have been developed over many years of experience. The important thing is to not let the building blocks of the past become the stumbling blocks of a greater future.

To his credit, our vice-president, bristling under an admonition from his boss to stop being defensive and embrace this new knowledge, began following our techniques to provide frequent feedback reinforcing the behavior he sought to have repeated. Within a month, the period-end financial reports indicated a little progress—not enough to elicit an acknowledgment of progress from the vice-president, but improvement nonetheless. We all recognized that although the techniques we had used always begin to work immediately, attitudes change slowly if at all. I have learned to let people learn at their own pace.

The following spring, on a return trip to this company's headquarters, I was confronted by the vice-president with his scorecard for the past ten periods. It showed a steady improvement in the shrink from the pre-installation level of more than 12 percent down to less than the 6-percent target established by management for the previous period (and originally thought unachievable by the division and store personnel). In fact, for the period just ended, the number was less than 5 percent, ranking this division among the top produce departments in the entire country! Yes, shrink was still a factor—there was still an asymptote of shrink. But it was closer to target for more of the stores, flatter and more consistent, and it still mirrored the level of unnecessary inventory. Also, the spikes on both scorecards were mitigated, and we were celebrating and rewarding behavior that resulted in performance vastly better than it used to be.

The vice-president approached me with a true "in your face, coach" mindset. Yes, he had been brought to task publicly for his resistance to learn and think, and he was after his pound of flesh. But the gleam in his eye told the real story of growth and learning, that he had learned to analyze the obvious and incorporate it into his personal and professional growth. I attempted to be solicitous with the comment, "That's real nice," which he countered with, "Nice! You say 'nice'? This scorecard annualizes to an additional $2.8 million dollars of gross profit that we spend nothing to generate, and it will become bottom-line profits in its entirety."

"Nice!" he continued. "That is a lot better than nice!" I had to agree, and I was, of course, extremely happy to do so.

On the front of your pocket calculator is a key that has both a plus sign and a minus sign on it, like this: +/-. A powerful little key, it turns a positive number into a negative, and a negative number into a positive, all at the touch of a finger. Similarly, when a problem is clearly defined and then restated in positive terms, it becomes a goal that leads to the solution of the problem. Suppose you've decided to buy a humble $500,000 home—your last child has left the nest, and you don't need your *big* house anymore. But the problem is, you don't know what $500,000 homes are available in your area. What's your goal? Turn the problem around: your goal is to find out what $500,000 homes are available in your area. Obvious, right? That's the point. Now think about your current problems that might become obvious goals if you just turn them around. In the heart of every clearly defined problem is the seed of its solution. Find it, and you will know what steps to take, even when the obvious doesn't seem so obvious.

COMMUNICATING THE OBVIOUS

4

THE POWER OF THE "PER"

hen Frank began his new position as director of
manufacturing at a bio-medical plastics extru-
sion company, the president told him that profits were low. Among other reasons, the president said, there was too much waste and
inefficiency on the press line. It didn't take Frank long to
confirm that observation. On his first day he watched the
press operators sweep the rejected plastic products into a
pile on the floor. The rejected product was then recycled by
grinding it into raw material. Frank knew from experience
that the waste from twenty-five presses shouldn't exceed
fifty pounds per day, but what he saw being swept up
looked to him like much more than fifty pounds.

Frank asked the press operators to weigh the scrap before it was reground. Then he asked one of the operators to
maintain a daily scorecard to track the total weight of the
scrap from all twenty-five presses. The scorecard was
posted daily on a bulletin board in the press room. The operators were immediately interested in the scorecard, and in
the first three weeks the amount of scrap decreased from
108 to 87 pounds per day. But the scrap plateaued between
80 to 90 pounds per day, and Frank knew that at least another 40 percent reduction was possible.

So Frank asked the press operator who was maintaining
the scorecard to add a second scorecard. This one, he said,

would track the amount of waste per employee labor hour per day. He said he wanted each employee to visually see how much waste he or she created every hour of every day. And he wanted to tie that number to labor, his largest controllable expense.

The new scorecard showed that, with 350 labor hours per day, there were 4.1 ounces of scrap for each employee labor hour each day. The new scorecard was posted, and it too triggered immediate interest among the press operators. Their interest, Frank observed, focused on how much product was represented by four ounces. That was because the biomedical products themselves were very small and lightweight, and it took several hundred items to equal four ounces. The operators were shocked to learn that each of them wasted four ounces (several hundred items) for each hour they operated a press every day.

Over the next two weeks, the press operators asked for permission to change a number of operational procedures in their department. The new procedures, along with some obvious performance improvements and a growing concern for quality, decreased the scrap per employee labor hour from 4 ounces to 2.65 ounces. In the following two weeks, it was further reduced to 2.13 ounces, which seemed to be a plateau. With obvious success, the press operators were jubilant and continued to look for additional methods of improving their efficiency.

Frank noted that 2.13 ounces of waste per employee labor hour equated to 46.6 pounds of scrap per day from the twenty-five presses, which was almost exactly what he had thought was possible on his first day as director of manufacturing. He estimated for me that the 51 percent decrease in waste per day represented a $135,000 net dollar savings to his company each year.

What do you see that's obvious in this illustration?

Why did Frank succeed?

Was he just lucky?

Or did he just stumble onto a solution?

The "per" in Frank's use of scorecards wasn't luck. He

didn't stumble onto the solution. It was a skill he had learned by understanding and using the "power of the per." He understood a principle in *The Game of Work* called "results to resource ratio." The "power of the per" is one of the greatest tools anyone can use—for business and for personal life. There is an incredible power in "pers" that can unlock employee motivation and focus attention on the business elements that drive success. But to understand what "pers" are and how we can use them to become more successful, we must first set the stage.

TODAY'S BUSINESS CLIMATE

In today's business world, it's not difficult to find people who go to work, punch the time clock, receive frequent negative comments from their boss, seldom receive positive or constructive comments from anyone, get a paycheck, go home feeling unfulfilled, and then feel threatened when they are summoned to an annual performance appraisal. It's also not uncommon to hear managers complain that too many employees lack motivation, enthusiasm, and commitment.

Yet after work, many of these "unmotivated" and "uncommitted" workers head to the bowling alley, baseball diamond, or favorite fishing hole and demonstrate all the motivation, enthusiasm, and commitment the managers would love to have at work. Why? How can people feel more commitment and enthusiasm at the bowling alley than at work?

The answer lies in the fundamental difference between the way most jobs have been set up and the way recreational sports have been set up: At the bowling alley, the players know if they are winning or losing. They receive instant feedback on their performance from an electronic scoreboard. The score tells them how they are doing compared to the other players, against an accepted standard, and against their own past performance. Bowlers know how they are doing from minute to minute. By contrast, most workers have to wait for the annual performance appraisal to find out if they are even playing the right game.

THE POWER OF SCOREBOARDS

Most recreational sports have scoreboards to keep track of the game score and the time remaining. Most professional sporting events have multi-million dollar scoreboards that keep fans current on virtually every aspect of the game. These huge scoreboards communicate up-to-the-minute information on players' performance, and some even show instant replays.

But where is the scoreboard at work? And if there were a scoreboard at work, what would it measure? How would the "score" be calculated? What would be the criteria for making "points"?

A traditional, autocratic manager might say that people ought to work on the job because they are paid to work. He or she might say that keeping score at work and even providing a scoreboard isn't necessary, because receiving a paycheck ought to be enough motivation by itself. But if scoreboards aren't necessary, why does the performance of so many workers skyrocket when a meaningful scoreboard is incorporated into their daily work routine? Why have literally thousands of people and organizations dramatically improved personal and organizational performance with the introduction of scorecards or scoreboards?

Unlocking the motivation of recreation in the workplace begins with establishing specific scorecards for each worker or team of workers. The scorecards must be visible and personal so each person can see "the score," the results of his or her daily performance. Not annually or semiannually, like performance appraisals. Not quarterly or monthly, like most financial statements. Not weekly, like departmental reports. Every work day. Daily feedback on work performance enables workers to know, at the end of each work day, if they are winning or losing. And that knowledge is the basis of self-motivation, the essence of job commitment, and the foundation of personal enthusiasm.

RESULTS TO RESOURCE RATIOS

There is a fool-proof seven-step process that Frank used to implement meaningful scorecards for his new company. It's called a Results to Resource Ratio (RRR), and it was first described as a business principle in my book *The Game of Work*. The power of the "pers" is tied directly to RRRs.

The principle of Results to Resource Ratios is not new. In fact, it has been used extensively in recreation and professional sports. In football, a running back has a personal scorecard that tracks yards per carry. In basketball, a player has a personal scorecard that tracks assists per game. In golf, a player has a personal scorecard that tracks shots per hole. In baseball, a pitcher has a personal scorecard that tracks strikes per inning.

The value of RRRs to both players and spectators is enormous. Players set goals to maintain certain levels of performance based on RRRs. The spectators cheer on the players, also based on specific RRR performance. And in professional sports, management has started to tie compensation to performance, based on RRRs.

We have used RRRs in business, largely without realizing or unlocking their motivational potential. Return On Investment (ROI), for example, is an RRR used in most businesses. The problem is that in a typical business organization, the ROI is kept secret; only a few privileged executives and managers are permitted to know how the company is actually doing. The majority of workers who have a direct impact on the ROI aren't permitted to even see it. That is like showing the box scores after a game to the coach but never to the players. In sports we would say that's crazy; regrettably, in too many businesses it's considered standard operating procedure.

THE SEVEN-STEP RRR PROCESS

You can establish your own RRRs for your job, your department, and your company. Divide a piece of paper into two columns by drawing a vertical line down the middle, from top to bottom. Label the left column "Results" and the right column "Resources."

Step 1. In the left column labeled "Results," list at least six results for which you are paid. Be sure to list specific, measurable results. Some people, when completing this exercise, tend to list duties associated with their job, so be sure to list specific results, such as profit, on-time delivery, or signed orders.

Step 2. In the right column labeled "Resources," list up to six of the most expensive resources you have available to accomplish your results. Resources are things that usually have a cost associated with them. They include such things as time, facilities, people, labor cost or hours, and space. Another way to think of resources is to identify your "opportunities." Each time you visit the gas station, you are an opportunity to the attendant and owner of the station. The amount of gas you purchase and the extent to which you purchase anything in addition to gas show how effectively the station capitalizes on the opportunity of having you make a purchase.

Step 3. Delete any item in your "Results" column that cannot be quantified or measured in specific numerical terms. Carefully consider each item to ensure that you know or can devise a method to measure improvement. For example, if you have "Improve Employee Attitudes" as one of your results, it should be deleted from the list, because there is no objective method to measure any change in employee attitudes. But if you have "Increase Profit" as a result, it should remain on your list, because "profit" is a measurable result. Make a brief note of how each item in your "Results" column can be measured or quantified.

Step 4. Delete any item in your "Resources" column that also cannot be quantified or measured in specific numerical terms. This typically isn't a problem, because most resources can be measured. Once again, make a note of how each item in this column can be measured or counted.

Step 5. Prioritize the results in the "Results" column by writing a "1" next to the most important result for which you are paid. Then write a "2" next to the second most important result, and so forth. Be sure to carefully identify your most important results. If you have a problem with this step or are unsure of your decisions, try sharing your list with a supervisor or colleague; second opinions often are helpful.

Step 6. Prioritize your resources in the "Resources" column by writing a "1" next to the most expensive resource. Then, place a "2" by the second most costly resource, and so forth. In most cases, the most costly resource will be the most important, but it may not be for you. Give this step some thought before going on.

Step 7. Now you can create a Results to Resource Ratio by drawing a line to connect your number-one result with your number-one resource. It might be something like Net Profit per Employee Labor Hour, or it could be On Time Reports per Month, or it could be Sales Presentations Made per Day. The key part of any RRR is the "per." The "per" creates the relationship between the result and the resource.

The two number-one items may or may not combine to form a meaningful RRR for you. If they don't, connect number-one result with number-two resource; then try number-two result with number-one resource. Then connect number two with number two, and so on. Create at least three

RRRs that together best describe the responsibilities for which you are accountable.

CREATING SCORECARDS FROM *RRRs*

The three RRRs you have selected can now be used to create scorecards to track your progress in those areas. Create a line graph for each RRR. If one element of an RRR is time, put it on the horizontal axis of the graph. Use the vertical axis of the graph for magnitude. (See the appendix for sample RRRs.)

DISPLAYING YOUR SCORECARDS

Just as the scoreboard in football or basketball must be visible to the players, so also must your scorecards be visible to you. There isn't much value in establishing RRRs and creating scorecards only to hide them in a folder, notebook, or file cabinet. Scorecards have an incredible impact on your daily behavior when they are placed where you can't hide from them. Most of our clients have learned that a scorecard hanging on the wall is a much stronger motivator than a scorecard hidden in a drawer. In fact, in a very bold move, a Canadian client of ours hung his three scorecards on his office door, facing the hallway, where all his employees could see his daily improvement (or lack thereof). The more visible, the better!

THE VALUE OF *RRRs*

Most people see a difference between "being measured" and "keeping a personal scorecard." Many people feel uncomfortable about being "measured" because they think the information might be used against them in a negative way. Scorecards, on the other hand, are usually not intimidating because they are positive and are inherently designed to show improvement in performance.

The introduction of scorecards based on meaningful RRRs has three important benefits. First, employees know exactly the results for which they are responsible. There is no question in anyone's mind about who is responsible for what results. Second, employees know they are accountable to their manager for the results. The process of establishing and maintaining scorecards is a great communicator of accountability. And third, because employees maintain their own scorecards daily, they develop a psychological ownership of both the results and the resources. This psychological ownership of results can be one of the most powerful tools available to any organization. Psychological ownership of resources helps players pay closer attention to the cost and use of organizational assets, including their own time.

We have witnessed numerous cases where the establishment of RRRs and scorecards has changed an organization that was heading toward disaster into one with a sound financial future.

Traditional methods of communicating feedback in an organization lack the ability to motivate players to superior performance. The power of the "pers" contains the secrets of true self-motivation; using the power of the "pers" gives you the ability to unlock that hidden power in your organization.

5

AGREEING ON THE OBVIOUS

S
everal years ago, I worked with a chain of twenty-five convenience stores. I started the project on a strong recommendation from the chain's bank and from other local business leaders. In an initial interview, the owner of the chain told me the company's executive committee already understood and believed the Game of Work philosophy. He insisted the key to improving the business was really very simple—the store managers just needed to be more committed. Trusting soul that I am, I believed him.

Even at the design-stage meeting with the CEO, I was lulled into a false sense of security and agreed to go along with a plan to have some of the store managers participate with the executive committee. So we began our meetings.

We proceeded into a world-class session of denial and excuse-making. Ordinarily our examination of a company's Results to Resources Ratios reveals the important behaviors for even the most reluctant manager. But not in this group. Every possible suggestion for scorekeeping and accountability was met with scorn and derision.

The company's *apparent* problem was that gross profit was way too low. So, naturally, I kept trying to convince them of two facts I have learned after more than two decades of consulting and four decades of working in the retail business:

1. You must increase the customer count, which also means customers are coming back because they are satisfied with your package of goods and services.

2. You must increase the amount of gross margin dollar per customer visit.

As I reviewed these two facts with the managers, the immediate wisdom of my experience was not as readily received as I had expected it would be. In fact, it was met with categorical rejection: "Chuck, you don't understand our business! There are lots of reasons we don't want the 'gas-only' customer coming into the convenience store and purchasing additional items."

"Oh, really?" I said. "Tell me more." Apparently we did not agree on what seemed completely obvious to me. And the worst part was that these concepts were also new to the president and the district managers (contrary to what the owner had initially told me). Consequently, I had no support for this radical departure from the same old way of doing business.

I started asking questions: "What if we increase the number of gas-only customers who come into the convenience store, where we have much higher gross margins? What if we increase the number of gallons purchased each time a person buys gasoline? Why do we insist that the managers control cash and inventory to less than a variance of .005 per month but not ask them to work on increasing the gross margin by an amount that could be several magnitudes of that number? Isn't your basic problem that gross profit is down? What does that suggest to you?"

I watched in amazement as the managers evaded the implications of my questions. At all costs, they were determined to protect the status quo. They had two perfectly good reasons for leaving things just the way they were: the amount of gas sold was controlled by the price, and there was no customer loyalty. The disturbing thing was that even though we could not agree on what needed to be done to save the company, we could continue to make zero progress just fine. (This kind of thinking and reaction needs further research by someone with more time and grant money than I have, but it is so prevalent as to be frightening.)

It soon (but not soon enough) became obvious that we had a complete lack of agreement. And the need to agree that we did *not* agree then became our first order of business. The great negotiators of the world understand this need and have expounded it often, yet it usually escapes the giants of management. We decided to suspend the sessions with the managers until we had achieved agreement among the executive committee on the obvious ways to win in their business. And that's when things finally began to work. No, we didn't get evangelical conversions overnight, but removing the managers gave the executive group greater freedom to change their thinking and then their actions.

We had to go back to the beginning, and it was more like an infantry battle than a nuclear air strike, with hard slogging for every foot, even every inch of concurrence. But it was well worth the effort. After a couple of meetings, we had established obvious ways the managers could win, and we had arranged these in order of importance. Our president was coming back to the basics of what had made the business, a second-generation affair, successful in the first place. Finally, we agreed that the company needed to do a better job of serving a larger percentage of the customer's total needs for the goods and services the company had chosen to sell.

Once we had agreed on the criteria of what constituted success for this company, we began to accumulate data on those criteria, and as soon as we got the first report, the inevitable comparisons began. Why did some of our data agree with our observations and some operate in what seemed to be direct contradiction of what we had thought to be true? How could we, in the same market, with the same cultural environment, get almost twice as much merchandise sales in one station as in another? Naturally, we had some great opinions on the subject, but we still had to begin to look for additional answers. At least we now agreed on what to look for, and, with the concurrence of the executive committee, the managers, too, began to accept the possibility and responsibility of change.

Common Sense

At any point in this experience, it would have been easy for me to give up and walk out the door. I was pretty sure I understood the situation correctly, so what was the matter with the other people in the deal? "Why can't they see it?" I asked myself, not once, but several times. "They just don't have any common sense." And that's usually what we say about people who don't agree with us.

But is common sense a given? Is it objective or subjective? Is it universal or situational? Is it inherited, or can it be learned? Is it dynamic or static? Does our common definition match or conflict with what we can agree common sense is under closer scrutiny?

I am afraid we behave and treat this concept as if it were:

1. Objective—a firm, unchanging principle.

2. Universal—once we have it, we always respond with common sense regardless of the situation.

3. Inherited or intuitive—something that should have been learned a long time before employment here began.

4. Static—once developed, it will never be lost and will remain in its present state throughout life.

Let's examine these assumptions. (Of course, you are free to agree or disagree as your experience dictates.)

Is common sense objective or subjective? If I demonstrate common sense to one member of the leadership in my organization, will the other leaders see my judgment in the same way? Will the controller see my upgrade to first class on my return flight (to enjoy four hours with a prime prospect I bumped into at the gate) as the same common-sense decision as does the sales vice-president I report to? If I don't sell the prospect, will the sales vice-president see it as a good decision anyway? Will the interpretation of my common sense depend on what total sales were for the period? If they were down, would it have been common sense to save the airfare or to spend the extra upgrade and attempt to get the business? In my opinion, common sense is subjective—in the eye of the beholder—which is why it is so often difficult to get agreement on what ought to be obvious.

What about universality? Some electricians do not disconnect the power while working on the wiring. Why? They believe that unless they are grounded, they are safe around 110-volt current. And besides, leaving the power on saves time on small adjustments. Other electricians always shut off the power until they complete the job and run another check. Maybe it's the number of jolts in the past that makes the difference.

In the Western world, we soak in soapy water and then rinse—common sense. In the Pacific Rim, common sense is that a person would never sit in water containing the dirt just washed from the body. There, people wash, rinse, and *then* relax in hot, clean water. As our world shrinks with electronic round-the-clock information, we are becoming more aware that what is common sense in Terre Haute is not necessarily common sense in Tangiers or Taiwan. I think examination here concludes that common sense is more situational than universal. And if we are trying to get agreement with someone from another culture, we need to try to see their perspective, to understand *their* common sense.

Is common sense inherited or learned? Popular opinion seems to be that it is inherited or developed at an early age. Or at least most of us think, "I don't care when my new recruits got their common sense as long as they got it before they came to work here." If you doubt that statement, poll your associates and ask, "Which of our employees have most increased their common sense during the past quarter?" No, we expect common sense to be in place prior to orientation, and with that assumption we preclude the possibility of helping develop that characteristic. I believe we hold to this belief to *avoid* the inherent responsibility of developing common sense in the members of our team. If we admit that common sense can be learned, then we have to face our responsibility to teach it. And with care and concern, common sense can and must be taught.

For example, college students on a personal scholarship from parents usually "have no common sense" about the value of money and other resources, but they somehow develop that common sense when they have to pay their own way after graduation.

Allow me to introduce a definition that I believe summarizes our most common attitude toward common sense: *People have common sense if they do what we would do if we were in the same situation.* Conclusion: common sense is dynamic, and beautifully so.

We must take up the gauntlet to teach common sense to the majority of our players and increase their capacities to perform. Why? *Because we cannot expect people to do what we would do unless they know what we know.* So, when we see people demonstrating a lack of common sense (by the above definition), we must first ask ourselves, "What do they *not* know that I *do* know that would help them improve?" Never assume that your players understand, or that they should have learned something before they were entrusted to you. Teach them, understand them, and, of course, trust them.

Also, take time to listen—one of the key ingredients in getting agreement on things. Often when we request performance from our players, they ask with their mouth or with their eyes, "Why should I?" or "What's in it for me?" How do we respond to these simple and, believe it or not, well-intentioned requests?

Do we accept these questions openly for what they are, as requests for more understanding or motivation or both? Such questions almost always reflect honesty, integrity, and trust. People really want to know! Unfortunately, too many managers ask the following question in response: "How long have you worked here? No, don't count tomorrow." Or the famous "Do you know who I am?" Most of us would have to admit to an initial defensive posture—one of threatened authority and some insecurity. We judge the questioner as insubordinate, not as a team player. This response is so prevalent among managers that employees usually ask such important questions only with their eyes, having learned long ago that asking with the mouth is not conducive to a long career.

Please think this through: *When players ask with their mouth or their eyes, "Why should I?" or "What's in it for me?" they are attempting to become more self-motivated, not insubordinate.* They are saying, "Increase my understanding, give me more of what you have, and I will be more like you in my performance." Give them the best you have, your experience, and you will find the agreement on the obvious much greater on your team and in your game.

HARDENING OF THE CATEGORIES

Part of the problem in getting people to agree on things is that they already have their own "world-view," their own way of thinking about things. An interesting experiment is to take twenty books from your bookshelf and ask ten different people to categorize them. Just ask the people to sort the books into various piles. The results of this experiment are fascinating. Some people categorize the books by subject. Some categorize them by author. Some do it by color. Some do it by size. You'll get all kinds of variations. Ask the people why they sorted the books the way they did, and you'll get some very interesting answers. Most people will say something like, "That was the most obvious way to do it." The fact is, most people do *not* think alike. Not only that, but their ways of thinking are usually pretty firmly set—something I call "hardening of the categories." And that's one reason why it's sometimes so difficult to get people to agree on things.

You see, Plato was smarter than Aristotle. Aristotle broke

everything down into categories, getting very specific and very *firm* about where everything fit, like the people who categorized the books. The problem is, if I don't accept your categories (or vice versa), we're never going to agree on which book goes where. Plato, on the other hand, avoided this whole problem by looking at the big picture. Rather than putting things into categories, he thought about the *characteristics* of things, all the characteristics that make things what they are.

For example, what makes a horse a horse? Well, it shares certain characteristics with all other horses—legs, hooves, ears, a mane, and a tail, among others. "What if I cut off my horses's tail?" you ask. "Isn't it still a horse?" Consider the definition of Platonism: "The philosophy of Plato, especially insofar as it asserts the ideal forms as an absolute and eternal reality of which the phenomena of the world are an imperfect and transitory reflection." (*American Heritage Dictionary of the English Language* [New York: American Heritage Dictionary, 1969], p. 1004.) So I would agree that your tailless horse is still a horse; it's just an imperfect and transitory one. But then, this is an imperfect and transitory world.

So if we're trying to get agreement, sometimes we need to stop arguing about what something *is* and start considering the "ideal forms" of the kind of thing we're looking at. If you're in a meeting where everybody else is saying "That's a table," and you're saying, "No, that's a desk," it might be wise for everyone to step back and agree on the general characteristics of desks and tables. Then it's usually easier to look at the characteristics of the specific item under discussion and get some kind of agreement about it. Besides, considering the "ideal forms" of things sometimes raises our thinking to levels we hadn't previously considered. We may come to realize that we don't need a desk *or* a table but a laptop computer instead.

This brings us to what may be the most important part of getting agreement, of reaching consensus. Many people play the agreement game as if it were a battle to be won, gritting their teeth and holding their mechanical pencils like bayonets, warding off any ideas but their own. "The only way we're going to get agreement on this deal," they say, "is if the other side sees things my way." The trouble with this game is that if everyone plays it, agreement is never reached.

Now, that doesn't mean you should just roll over and play dead in order to get agreement. In fact, that's probably every bit as counterproductive as the "hold the line" mentality, because it means the tough guys always win. If you're tough, you may think that's okay. But then what happens if your position turns out to be wrong? What happens if you make a mistake? Maybe you could have learned something if you had just listened. Maybe you could have come out farther ahead. Would you rather succeed, or would you rather be right? I'd rather succeed, every time.

That doesn't mean I just "give in" to my "opponent." It means I work very hard at getting into a partnership that is willing to explore *every possibility that we can.*

One way to do that is to have the other person write down his or her position as completely and clearly as possible. On another piece of paper, write down your position in the same way. Trade pieces of paper and take turns reading each others' positions out loud until you both understand (not agree on) both positions. Then take those two pieces of paper and seal them in an envelope. Finally, get out some more paper—lots of it—and together write down *every other possible option or position but the two that are sealed in the envelope.*

In getting agreement, far too often we see things only as black or white. But there's a lot of gray between those two extremes. And let's not forget about red and green and orange and blue, and yellow with lavender spots. There's a whole rainbow of possibilities out there if we're just willing to look at it. Somewhere in that spectrum, we're likely to find the perfect solution for everyone, a solution that far surpasses all our preconceived ideas.

Also, let's not get trapped in the notion that we have to

make a decision once for all time. We can take an idea and try it for a while. If it works, great! If not, we can try something else. Have a little flexibility and creativity. Learn to be an explorer and an experimenter rather than a warrior. As you do, you'll find yourself and your team coming up with things you never would have dreamed of in the past. You'll learn what it really means to get agreement on the obvious.

6

KEEPING THE OBVIOUS IN MIND

I once worked with a company that had teetered on the brink of bankruptcy for two years, kept afloat only by the personal assets of the founder (the father of the current management) who had socked away some cash in more prosperous times. Several things were obvious: cash flow was off, order productivity was atrocious, and backlog was nonexistent. As we looked around, we wondered what had happened. How could this company, with a solid product in adequate demand, fall into such decay and disrepair? On our third visit to the plant, I noticed a curious contraption tucked away in the corner of the board room. It was a display rack, similar to those in poster shops, designed to display a sample of each kind of the company's rolled stock. What was in the display rack? Scorecards, on each of the key areas we were trying to improve. Closer investigation revealed that the most recent information on the scorecards was two years old. Funny—that was when the company's decline had begun. After further questioning, we learned that the operations officer had stopped keeping the scorecards because they had made the company look bad, and he hadn't wanted to be embarrassed in board meetings—especially since the board included Mom and Dad. How much better things might have been if he had maintained front-of-mind awareness of the company's problems and taken action to correct them. He *knew* what was important, but he had turned his back on it. He had failed to keep the obviously important things in mind.

FRONT-OF-MIND AWARENESS

A great chief executive told The Game of Work he had never seen a bad graph posted. In an off-handed fashion, he was confirming the principle of front-of-mind awareness. He said that either the scorecard (the graph) would eventually reflect the player's improvement, or the player would try to remove the scorecard from public (and, more important, personal) view. If we keep score, we are guaranteed to win more often. The simple existence of a scorecard that provides feedback about our performance to ourselves and the world encourages us to behave so that our results move to match our stated values.

Keeping the obvious in mind ought to be easy. After all, what is obvious is *obvious*, right? But have you ever forgotten your wedding anniversary? How about your daughter's dance recital? What about that important meeting with the boss? *Why* we forget such important things is something of a mystery, perhaps best left to the cogitations of the psychiatrist. But remembering the important things, both in business and in everyday life, is central to managing the obvious. In managing the obvious, we use a concept called "front-of-mind awareness," which is the thing that makes grooms forget their lines at the wedding, drop the ring, and not be able to eat at the reception. Front-of-mind awareness makes it nearly impossible to be distracted by items other than our primary objective. Front-of-mind awareness is a goal much to be desired. It breeds commitment, focus, and results. It helps us remember what is important. It helps us recall, when we are up to our necks in alligators, that our original objective was to drain the swamp.

THE POWER OF FEEDBACK

I believe we have a psychological and even physiological need to receive feedback constantly. In fact, I believe that the denial or withholding of feedback is the most severe form of psychological punishment one can inflict on another human being.

In our penal system, we call the withholding of feedback "solitary confinement." The first step in brainwashing is isolation, combined with the disruption of normal bodily functions—anything to break up the body's feedback system and upset psychological equilibrium. In the military academies, ostracized cadets are given the "silent treatment," and those who have been subjected to it have changed their behavior or left the academy. In many religions, the withholding of feedback is referred to as being shunned, disfellowshipped, or excommunicated, and every major religion has its way of separating the wayward from the faithful flock. Around the house, we may simply say our husband or wife "is on one today" and refuse to talk with him or her. Even at the office, if I refuse to participate in the normal morning banter of greeting and exchanging pleasantries, I am labeled a malcontent and left out of the luncheon invitation that day.

An experiment was conducted several years ago in an attempt to mellow out the type-A personality. Remember the flotation chamber? It was a seven-foot-long sarcophagus that contained about a foot of saltwater to ensure that the subject would have little sense of gravity. It was warmed to human body temperature to lessen the sense of touch. White noise was played through the underwater speakers, and, of course, all light was shut out to eliminate visual stimulation. Every sense was neutralized, every feedback system rendered inactive. The intent was to temporarily remove all the cares of the world and provide a sense of security. The result? The subjects became paranoid and neurotic. Total separation from the outside world does not produce relaxation but rather disorientation. This kind of process, taken to its extreme for extended periods of time, is the first step in the interrogation process used by the modern intelligence community.

Yes, the withholding of feedback is the most severe form of psychological punishment you can inflict on someone—except in the American management system, where it is considered standard operating procedure!

Ask yourself, "Am I unintentionally, or even intentionally, denying any of the members of my team feedback that would enhance their performance or enjoyment of the job?" Then ask yourself, "Would I or any of my team accept the frequency of feedback off the job that we live with, albeit unhappily, on the job?"

How powerful is feedback? A professor of social psychology became the victim of her students when she was about ten minutes late for class. The professor was a pacer, and, in her absence, the students agreed that when she moved toward the door, they would show little interest in the class. When she moved toward the window, they would be eager and attentive learners. When the professor finally got to class, the students carried out their scheme. Soon the professor was rooted to the window, quite pleased at the students' responsiveness to her lecture. In less than an hour, an expert's behavior was modified—and we believe we can get by with an annual performance review. (See Mildred Newman and Bernard Berkowitz, *How to Take Charge of Your Life* [New York: Bantam Books, 1978], pp. 43-44.)

If you don't think feedback is important, try counting the mirrors at your house. If you don't think feedback is important, try ignoring your preschooler. Ever try? "Come see what I built in the garage!" "No, I'm reading the paper." "But I want you to see what I built!" "No, I'm busy." What is the next sound you are likely to hear? The sound of a hacksaw blade being applied to a leg of the dining-room table. That child is going to get some feedback! And if you doubt the need for feedback, try telling the special person in your life that the outfit he or she has picked out for the company Christmas party is just "okay."

The higher the uncertainty level of the employee, the higher the need for feedback. Also, the more important the giver of feedback is in the eyes of the recipient, the more important the need for feedback.

ACCENTUATE THE POSITIVE

Behavior you wish to have repeated must be reinforced. That is probably the oldest and most obvious principle of feedback, and yet it is undoubtedly the most ignored and abused. Do you, when coaching your team, talk about the orders that were shipped complete and the projects that were finished on time, or do you talk about how many times you have been out of stock and the dozens of projects that were late? What obvious thing do you need to keep in mind? The behavior you want repeated—*not* the behavior you didn't want in the first place.

Consider the child who brings home a report card with two C's, three D's, and an F. How much feedback does that child receive? And what is the emotional intensity of that feedback? "You idiot! How could you embarrass us this way? Now I'll have to take time off from work and go down to see your teacher. How could you do such a thing?" We give lots of strokes, lots of attention, but attention to the wrong things. And if the child gets the message and returns with two A's, three B's, and only one C, what do we say? "Well, it's about time." Then we wonder why the child does poorly in school for the rest of the year. What we are telling the child is, "If you are lonely, just mess up, and we'll get you all of the attention you can stand." We fail to reinforce the positive behavior we want repeated.

The whale trainers at Sea World are smarter than most managers. You may have observed that it is not natural behavior for a ten-ton whale to leave the sanctuary of the water and jump twenty-two feet over a rope. But the trainers are very special people, and along with communicating to the whales that they care and have the whales' best interests at heart, they make a most important decision that we often overlook in business—they decide what they want the whales to do. It's very simple: jump over the rope. Then they begin to construct circumstances that will reinforce the behavior they seek to have repeated. They put the rope at a level where the whale can't possibly fail—on the bottom of the tank. When the whale swims over the rope, they feed it. Over several months, they gradually move the rope upward, continuing to reward the whale for its successes, until it is making those spectacular leaps that audiences love to watch. How fast do they raise the rope? Slowly enough that the whale doesn't starve.

Can you imagine the classical managerial approach to this problem? First we put the rope twenty-two feet above the water and call it goal-setting. Then we take the kettle of fish up to the level of the rope—"Incentive motivation," we say. Then we shout, "Jump, whale, jump!" If our whale doesn't respond, we scream a little louder with even more enthusiasm. After a period of nothing happening, we scold the whale for staying on the bottom of the tank, where it naturally belongs. Finally we conclude, "What a dumb whale!" If we have a human resources department, we blame the shortsightedness of the collegiate recruiting program or other circumstances for the whale continuing to do what it has done all its life—stay in the safe, cool water. And, of course, we probably don't have much of a show.

Fortunately for those of us who enjoy watching whales jump, the trainers at Sea World do better at keeping the obvious in mind. The result is wonderful to behold—whales that leap twenty-two feet out of the water, to the astonishment of the spectators and the gratification of the trainers. No doubt the whales enjoy it too.

Obvious principles? Sure. But how often do we follow them in business?

Do we clearly define the goals we want our employees to achieve and then help them keep those goals in mind by providing frequent feedback? Or do we merely assign them certain tasks, perhaps without even telling them the reasons for doing the tasks? Then, later, do we forget about what we assigned? If *we* don't keep the obvious in mind, how can we expect our players to do it?

A doughnut store manager came to one of our training sessions on how to manage the obvious with a story on his mind. "You won't believe it," he said. "You just won't believe it." I love to hear these words from our clients because when I do, I know I'm going to hear a wonderful new example of the greatness of people in the work force. I was not to be disappointed this time, either.

"It was about eight o'clock in the morning," he continued, "and I saw our doughnut frier sitting in the restaurant having a cup of coffee after completing his midnight-to-dawn shift. 'John,' I said, 'do you know the bakery sales goals for today?' Without batting an eyelash, he recited the amount of the sales, the desired customer count, and the average customer purchase amount. Then he blew me away by adding the desired labor required to accomplish those goals. 'John, that is just great, simply great!' I said, beaming. I was attempting to reinforce the behavior we wanted repeated. I was truly ecstatic with this front-line awareness."

"My joy was soon jolted by a dose of reality, however. Buoyed by my new openness and enthusiasm, John ventured to ask a question of me. 'Mr. Larson,' he asked with positive expectation in his voice, 'do you know the goals for tomorrow?' Right then I realized that I didn't know the goals. Here I was preaching, but I was not practicing what I preached. Embarrassed, I confessed my shortsightedness to John and resolved never to be without the information that had become so important to my players. If they needed to keep the obvious in mind, so did I."

TWO DENTISTS WHO FORGOT THE OBVIOUS

A few years ago, I consulted with two partners in a dental practice. They were struggling along on about $300,000 a year in total practice revenue—not a very good income for one dentist and catastrophic when divided between two of them. Even though the senior partner was not completely dependent on the practice for his living, this was a problem that needed to be solved. We negotiated a standard "design-stage" meeting to test the character of the players and determine how in tune with the reality of their situation they were and what obvious problems we could agree on. In dentistry, as in many other businesses and almost all service industries, gross revenue is a product of the number of customers served and the magnitude of that service in dollars.

The initial assessment of these dentists was that in this little town (population of five thousand with another five thousand in the rural area around it), there simply were not enough patients available to them, so nothing could be done about their miserable lot. A typical response—all too frequently we look at the gross dollars of a business and never delve into the underlying elements that provide those dollars. I persisted in my questioning: "How much do you generate from each patient visit?" "About seventy dollars," came the answer, "but there aren't enough patients in this area to make a difference. What do you suggest we do—bus in patients from the next county?" "Maybe," I said, "but let's see who's *here* first. How many patient visits did you have last month?" They had performed the requisite assortment of cleanings, fillings, and rechecks, with an occasional emergency thrown in for good measure. Nothing unusual so far. But in the Game of Work, we use the Results to Resources Ratio, which helps us look for the *untapped* resources in a business. Remember, we simply list *all* the business's resources and analyze and prioritize them to see what previously unrecognized opportunities exist for using them to improve our results.

In looking for resources, I asked, "How many files for past patients do you have?" "We don't know," they said. "We've never counted." "Let's count," I said. And we did, learning that the dentists had about fifteen hundred past patients. Now, what obvious fact does every child know about how often we need to visit the dentist? *Twice a year.* The trouble was, these dentists had failed to keep the obvious in mind. But with renewed awareness, they realized that they needed three thousand patient visits a year just to maintain appropriate dental hygiene for their clients. And to get that, they simply needed to mail them a reminder notice twice a year. Of course, not all of the patients responded (people tend to put off going to the dentist even when they are reminded of the opportunity), but enough did respond to raise the partnership's income to the level where it needed to be.

A MULTI-DEPARTMENT GROCERY STORE

I worked with a multi-department grocery store that was a wonderful example of failing to keep the obvious in mind. They were concerned only with the total sales dollars for the store, overlooking the opportunity to improve performance in each department. Like many other grocery stores, they even measured the effectiveness of their *overall* marketing efforts by tracking the percentage of total sales dollars from each of the different departments. This myopic approach has several limiting factors, among them:

1. It assumes there is only one resource "pie" to be divided among all the departments.

2. It implies competition among departments where none really exists.

3. It provides a number of prearranged excuses for non-performance, depending upon the promotional emphasis of the week.

4. It does not even allow the featured department to achieve its potential, because the method of evaluation does not focus on the potential the department could have achieved but rather on comparison with other departments.

To further complicate the lack of keeping the obvious in mind, the results were reviewed on the beginning of the week *following* the week of performance. What was wrong with that? At that point, *the game was over.* Even if a department was successful, the recognition and celebration of the effort occurred during the next set of circumstances, which were so different from the previous ones that no one could depend on repeating the success.

What could we do to solve the problem? We began with the exercise of the Results to Resources Ratio and determined that we were looking for an increase in *profit per customer visit.* Further reasoning showed that the department manager could not control all the expenses that affect net profit, so we constructed a scorecard for the *contribution before overhead and profit.* That would be figured on the gross margin dollars from the department and on expenses that could be controlled by the department manager, such as labor, supplies, and shrink (waste).

We believed we could calculate these figures daily, thereby living up to one of our keystone principles: *You can accomplish more in seven hours and forty-five minutes of work and fifteen minutes of scorekeeping than you can with eight hours of unscored activity.* And, of course, once the figures were calculated, we needed to keep the obvious in mind by displaying them to one and all. (After all, in sports they even let the defensive players look at the scoreboard.) Scorekeeping must be *highly visual*—get it up on the wall and keep it there. So each manager found a place in the immediate work area where all the players could see the scorecard.

GET THEM UP AND KEEP THEM UP

How important is sharing the information with the team? One of our clients in a regular follow-up meeting handed me a packet and said, "Here's what scorekeeping means to us, now that we've got it back and are doing it right. This is two million bucks." And I said, "Thanks, Dick. Is there a commission with it?" Then he told me the story: "We went through *The Game of Work*, we had some management changes, and we had a few people move around. Our first fiscal quarter operating statements came back $500,000 net profit below plan."

"We were still profitable and have always been a good

company, but $500,000 below plan over thirteen weeks in six supermarkets? That's not good."

"Coincidental to that experience, one night I picked up *The Game of Work* to re-read it, and I realized as I was reading that I had not seen the scorecards up in our stores. When we went through the implementation process, we had great participation and acceptance from our people, and we had five scorecards per manager across the board. These were active people who were responding to the scorecards just the way you said they would.

"The thought haunted me. That night, instead of attempting to sleep (which would have been hard to do anyway), I got into my car and drove to five of the six stores. I couldn't find the scorecards, or very few of them. I remember being warned that one of the riskiest times during scorekeeping is when a scorecard is filled up, because the temptation is to not put up the next edition. I made a commitment then to go back, get them up, and keep them up."

"Great story," I said.

"You haven't heard the best part," he replied. "The best part was what we did with our managers. We brought them together and shared with them what I had learned. Then we put the scorecards up and agreed to keep them up. Since then, we've gone through two more fiscal quarters. We are back on our budget and back on the plan. These scorecards I'm sharing with you, Chuck, represent $2,000,000 of increased operating net profit this year. We did this because we got them up and kept them up."

Then he made one of the great client statements (and there have been many) that have come out of years of implementing obvious principles. He said, "*I have never seen a bad scorecard up.* Either the player will improve the score, or the scorecard will be taken off the wall; but I have never seen a bad scorecard up. I know that, as a CEO, if I could get the commitment to keep the scorecards and feedback in front of my people, they have the character, the talent, and the will to win, grow, and progress. *I just need to get them up and keep them up.*"

KEEPING SCORE

The first rule of scorecards is that they have to be *relevant.* In the multi-department grocery store, we made the scorecards compare Tuesday to Tuesday, Thursday to Thursday.Why? Because people tend to shop on certain days (Saturday being the all-time favorite). This gave us the greatest chance for a relevant comparison between shopping days and an opportunity to increase the volume from week to week for any particular day.

The second rule of scorecards is that they must be *credible.* They have to display information about the things that are obviously important, and the information must be accurate and up to date. But beyond accuracy, it must be credible in the eyes of the player responsible for it.

The most important advantage of keeping the obvious in mind is that all of the players on the team are focused— and that's what we started to see in this grocery store. We started hearing about part-time or entry-level employees reacting to the daily scorecard with increased customer courtesy, increased creativity to achieve the marketing goals, and increased judgment on customer-sensitive marketing decisions—all of which affected our ability to achieve our goals.

We continued with the analysis, looking for the obvious ways we could succeed with each of these multi-department managers. For example, they could each increase the amount of business from each customer visit—*sales per customer.* While this is a traditional measurement, it is seldom reviewed daily, and even less frequently for only the customers who actually visit the department.

We could also reach our goals by increasing the total number of customers who visited a department and made any purchase at all. This became known as our customer penetration number, and it gave us useful information on the effectiveness of our entire merchandising program in attracting customers, once we had them in the store.

We continued to ask, "How does this department win?"

reasoning that control of major expenses against the major resources of opportunity would provide additional insight. We finalized this as *customers served per employee labor hour.* With all of these criteria, we persisted in the daily comparisons, but only of the department with itself—*not* with other departments. This gave each department a way to be victorious, to concentrate on the things that were controllable, and, if not controllable, at least subject to influence. Keeping the obvious in mind created more focus on what could actually be done, and it left little time for worrying about the other departments, which could not be controlled. Are you familiar with the Serenity Prayer?

> God, grant me the serenity to accept the things I cannot change, courage to change the things I can, and wisdom to know the difference.

Certainly things worth thinking about for anyone in business.

IGNORING THE UNIMPORTANT

As a young management trainee, I learned a valuable lesson about losing focus on the obvious. About ninety days into my first post-college employment, I was in the office of my mentor, Bob. Bob was successful, you could tell—he was a vice-president before the age of thirty-five, he had gray hair, he was an alumnus of my alma mater, and his personal secretary balanced his personal checkbook. What greater indications of success could there be?

Having a mentor program gave us young turks access to a higher level of learning than we would ordinarily have enjoyed, and I decided to take advantage of such a benefit. I was a "junior management trainee" in this company, and my life was being made miserable by the realities of the working world. So, I went to get consolation from my role model, obviously in an attempt to gain sympathy and some sense that I was all right in spite of my problems. "So what is the problem?" he generously asked. Then, of course, I let it all hang out: the competition had made my initial idea for world conquest look juvenile, the department that didn't report to me was uncooperative, the government had placed obstacles of incredible proportion in my path, I had no access to the executive washroom, and, to top it all off, the weather wasn't cooperating either. Oh, woe is me, I continued. (Of course, now I understand that such behavior is really an attempt to inflate the size of the problem beyond anything a mere mortal could be expected to handle. It's a fundamental excuse for nonperformance.)

In his wisdom, my mentor asked a pointed question: "What can you do about that?" "Well, nothing," I replied, my knee-jerk reaction exposing my motive in painting the grim scenario in the first place. "Good," he said. "Then why don't you?" "Why don't I what?" I asked. His reply: *"Do nothing. Don't commiserate about it, don't worry about it, don't even think about it. And don't come in here asking me for sympathy about it."* Then, before I could state a rebuttal, he continued, "Now, with all the extra time you will have, focus on the things you *can* influence, and make them make a difference."

I learned more about time management, personal responsibility, and success in two minutes at that mentor's knee than I had in all of my previous four years of post-high-school education. I learned the need to ignore the things that don't matter, and the importance of keeping the obvious in mind.

7

THE OBVIOUS SOURCE OF AUTHORITY

harlie Nash, the founder of American Motors, got his start with General Motors and later had a falling out with the company, which is when he left to start his own. Several years later, someone who was not real bright thought it might be nice to have Charlie come back and address a gathering of GM dealers about customer service. Charlie happily did so, and this (paraphrased) is part of what he said: "When I was a farm boy growing up in Wisconsin, my dad came to me with an old milk cow and said, 'Son, I'd like you to take this cow down to Farmer Jones.' I said, 'Fine, Dad. What do I do with her when I'm down there?' He said, 'Well, I want you to take her down and have her serviced.' Being about twelve years old and very curious about the world, I asked, 'What does it mean to have a cow serviced?' My dad got a funny look on his face and said, 'Why don't you ask Farmer Jones when you get there?' I obediently took hold of the rope and led the cow down to Farmer Jones. Then I said, 'Farmer Jones, my dad asked me to bring this cow down and have her serviced. What does it mean to have a cow serviced?' Farmer Jones got the same funny look as my dad, and he said, 'I really think it would be best if your father told you about that.' Realizing that neither one of them was going to tell me, I walked around to the back of the barn where a piece of board was missing and learned for myself what it meant to have a cow serviced. And that, I believe, is exactly the kind of service GM is giving its customers, which is why American Motors is going to be a force in the automobile business in the United States."

Do Charlie's words apply to us? Are we committed to customer satisfaction, or are we merely committed to customer service? Robert Townsend says that customer service is what we try when customer satisfaction has failed. He also says, "Get rid of the customer service department." Why? Because keeping customers satisfied is the responsibility of every member of the team—not of some mid-level manager in the corporate offices.

THE AUTHORITY OF THE CUSTOMER

Why are we seeing such an emphasis on the need for customer satisfaction? For an obvious reason that is often overlooked: customers are a source of authority for everyone in business, the most important source of all. Without customers, a business could not exist. It is the customers who dictate with their dollars what the company sells and how it sells it. If the president of your company came in to see you, wouldn't you do all in your power to serve him or her well? Then isn't it obvious how we need to treat our customers? And shouldn't those who serve the customers directly—the clerks on the showroom floor—have the authority to bring down all the powers of management to satisfy the customer's needs? Obviously, authority must be based on what needs to be done—not on arbitrary delegation. And we need to do a better job about finding out what needs to be done.

It is the exceeded expectation that is the source of true customer satisfaction, and the best of the best exceed the customer's expectation by going beyond the obvious with their customer surveys and needs polling. You may have heard of car companies who write to ask about your satisfaction with the car you bought from them. But please notice that they do so only when the car is less than one year old. Of course, you like it now. But I keep wondering who might have the courage to write when the car is five years old and not yet paid for and you're $2,000 upside down as the result of an unrealistic financing package. That's the kind of question we need to think about.

The satisfied customer knows that things just feel right, and the wise executive knows that feelings are facts. My wife, Carla, and I ate at a great little restaurant at Crested Butte, Colorado, and I looked around at what gave the place that certain something. There were ferns hanging from the ceiling, beautiful Christmas wreaths in the corners (this was late February), a salad bar that was stunning in its variety, a twenty-three-foot floor-to-ceiling view of the mountain, a great waiter who constantly but unobtrusively checked on our needs, and superb cuisine. I don't know which part made the difference, but altogether it felt real good.

How do we get the satisfaction level of the customer to rise? I believe we need to create a way to check our progress and maintain our commitment. If the presence of a daily scorecard will bring our behavior in any area closer to our stated values, then what better application for a scorecard than customer satisfaction? The challenge, in some people's minds, is how to define and quantify people's feelings about what we do. This is an appropriate concern. To address it, let's consider what we hear people saying about their satisfaction level. Then let's rank those responses on a report card, with grades ranging from A to F. It's easiest to begin with the extremes:

The A grade: "You *must* try . . . " We have all heard this or said it about the level of satisfaction we have received from a product or service. Think about the circumstances in which you have used this phrase to describe your feelings. Whether you were thinking of a tailor, a soup mix, or a world-class resort, your satisfaction level was indicated by your willingness to aggressively recommend the product or service to others without being asked.

The F grade: "Whatever you do, don't . . . " On the

other end of the spectrum is the experience we wouldn't wish on our worst enemy. Our intensity is equal to or maybe even greater than that of level A but in the opposite direction. We may be suing to recover costs, or we may be so offended we will never again darken the door of the establishment, but we are not suffering in silence. We are aggressively seeking to reduce the revenues of the offending business or product.

Other levels of customer satisfaction can be defined in the spectrum between the two extremes. You may want to define your own points or borrow these from some of our most customer-sensitive clients:

B: "Yes, I'd recommend it." Customers at this level will respond positively and even enthusiastically *if asked*, but they are not going around giving you free advertising. Still, they will give you high marks and can be relied upon for support when needed. This may be just a difference in the personality of the customers, but I doubt it. Haven't we all seen the meek become disciples when their expectations were more than exceeded?

C: "I got what I paid for." In this case, the goods and services were adequate. I was hungry and the cheeseburger filled me up. My car was broken when I brought it into the shop, and it was fixed when I drove it away. This level really does equate with a grade of C on a school report card: average performance. Sadly, in many business establishments customer satisfaction seldom even meets this basic level.

D: "I'm not really satisfied, but what can I do?" The inverse of level B, level D is where customers will respond negatively *if they are asked*. In some ways, this is the saddest—and the scariest—level of all. If disappointed customers would actively express their disapproval to others, we might at least hear about the problem eventually. But customers at this level don't do that. These are the customers who just never come back. I'm thinking of a restaurant that opened in our area a few years ago. It was advertised as the greatest thing since sliced bread, but when Carla and I tried it, we found the service less than adequate and the food about the same. "Maybe they're just having a bad day," we said. "Let's come back after they've had a chance to get their feet on the ground." A month later we tried them again—no change. We didn't complain to anyone, because the restaurant wasn't all that *bad*. It just wasn't very *good*. And after that, we never went back again. I guess other people had similar experiences, because a year later the restaurant closed. "Why didn't you tell them, Chuck?" you may be asking. Well, we just didn't. And that's what *defines* this level of satisfaction—or dissatisfaction. How can you avoid falling into the C, D, or F level of satisfaction? The obvious: *ask* your customers how you are doing.

JUST ASK

A good example is the CEO of a regional supermarket chain who identified, through a unique tracking/scorekeeping system, the company's top five hundred shoppers and then demographically and geographically selected twenty-five of them to invite to a brunch. He asked these customers such obvious questions as "What do you like?" "What do you not like?" "If you owned this business, what would you change?" He was so impressed with the usefulness of the answers that he established a toll-free customer hot line—to his office, not to the customer service department. (He must have followed our advice and re-read *Up the Organization*, by Robert Townsend.) He learned more about customer satisfaction in two months than anyone else had in the two-generation history of the company. The most incredible benefit was the increase in supervisory staff (twenty-five shoppers with a hot line to the chief stockholder are a powerful force), who told their friends that they could get what they wanted. This built the business and brought in some of the strongest customers in the world: those who are presold by the very people with whom they have the most in common.

Making Customers Feel Important

I remember being impressed by the creativity of a major Southern California retailer who would send out, ahead of the newspaper ads, a special pre-sale invitation. It allowed the holder to shop the back room—that's right, the back room—the place behind the door where the poor interior designer would never allow anyone. There were hundreds of customers lined up in single file because fire regulations controlled the number of people allowed at one time in this non-public area. Whether they knew it or not, they were there to purchase the same shoes that were available in the comfort of the fitting showroom. But the obvious principle here is that people want to be made to *feel important,* even if it means they have to climb over dusty, bare-wood shelving. This retailer is currently a flagship in one of the most respected retailing holding companies in the world. And I am sure those lines into the back room exist today—long lines of satisfied customers.

Authority within the Organization

On July 4, 1776, Thomas Jefferson and his associates declared: "We hold these truths to be self-evident; that all men are created equal; that they are endowed by their creator with certain unalienable rights; that among these are life, liberty, and the pursuit of happiness; that to secure these rights, governments are instituted among men, *deriving their just powers from the consent of the governed."*

Yet in business, we traditionally use authority to force employees to do what *management* requires, often ignoring the fact that our employees, much like our customers, are ultimately the source of managerial authority. Too often, we ignore their opinions and legitimate concerns for the betterment of the company or the customer or both.

We have created various cliches to back up this prehistoric position, such as the golden rule: "He who has the gold makes the rules." It has been said that "power corrupts and absolute power corrupts absolutely." I believe our incorrect perception of the source of power is the cornerstone of its abuse.

The traditional relationships of authority are mirrored in cartoons like the Jetsons, the Flintstones, and, of course, Blondie, in which Dagwood Bumstead is eternally kicked around the office by his hard-nosed boss, Mr. Dithers. Everywhere, we see ownership portrayed as the real source of authority, with no consideration for the rights of the people involved. The roots of slavery, colonialism (regardless of political persuasion), and, I am afraid, even the growing national disgrace of spouse and child abuse are extensions of this inappropriate assumption.

THE EROSION OF AUTHORITY

Some may argue that the abuse of authority comes from the willingness of subordinates to accept it. Much of the authority in an abusive system comes from the physical superiority or military might of the leader or leader group. Interestingly enough, we have seen an erosion of these power bases in the past three decades. Why? Because, I believe, the holders of the authority forgot the eternal nature of the bargain: that with authority comes a commensurate stewardship for the group over which they have authority. And if they violate the trust of that bargain, the authority will be stripped, probably by the group being governed or managed.

This is often seen, tragically, in families. A soaring divorce rate is evidence that people will no longer submit to the abuse of authority. Parents say things like, "As long as you live in this house . . . " Then we wonder why we have so many runaways. Even an explanation of power such as "Because I'm the mom, that's why" reinforces this belief system. But is biological coincidence really the source of parental authority? Something to think about.

Today we are even seeing the growth of rights groups representing people who have been abused by the inappropriate application of power. The rights of the elderly, for example, are represented by the American Association of Retired Persons, which is the largest lobbying group in American government. We are also hearing much about victims' rights from those who are tired of the misuse (or the nonuse) of the authority given to our judicial system.

Internationally, the fall of the Berlin Wall is an eloquent testimonial of the resolution of the abuse of authority. In Manilla, a longstanding dictator was reduced to exile when his abuse became great enough to stir the people to action. Even the roots of American government, the greatest democracy the world has ever known, are traceable to the abuse of authority by the British crown. The students of Tienemen Square in Beijing in the summer of 1989 made their statement about authority, a statement that will live in memory for instigators of far greater changes to come. And, like the freedom fighters on the streets of Budapest who did not see the realization of their dream until thirty-four years had passed, the students will not forever be silenced, and their cause will not die.

Where such statements of discontent are addressed in time, leadership can change if it is sufficiently enlightened. Too often, however, the expressions are withheld until the passion required to bring forth change is so great that the leadership must be replaced to satisfy the offended group.

This message is obvious. When a group senses enough abuse, it seeks to retract the authority it has granted. Look at how that principle would work in your business. What if there were a rights group for the people you manage? How would they see you? What would they tell you?

It has been said that unions flourish when management fails to meet the needs of the workers. This is true, and we have several examples of deunionization occurring where workers rights become reestablished. *The obvious principle is that authority comes from the groups for whose benefit it is to be used:* children, employees, customers, church members; the Little League baseball, basketball, or football team. And any time those parents, managers, salespeople, leaders, preachers, or coaches forget the true source of authority, they sow the seeds of defeat for their groups and their mission objectives. Obvious, right? Then why do we have so many examples of people who have ignored this principle? The answer lies in the human tendency to get by, to give just enough to meet the minimum performance standard. This was given us in the negative conditioning we received as children and continue to receive from altogether too many of our managers today. As one nineteenth-century leader noted, "We have learned by sad experience that it is the nature and disposition of almost all men, as soon as they get a little authority, as they suppose, they will immediately begin to exercise unrighteous dominion."

THE RIGHT TO MANAGE

Authority, then, when freely given, becomes more of a "right to manage" or a right to serve. And, like all other rights, it is subject to recall from the grantor. Perhaps the best way to check on where you are with your grantors and how you are discharging your stewardship is to demonstrate a continuous program of needs assessment and execution. We have seen many successful executions of consumer panels and group-change assessments. These must be balanced against the management responsibility for long-range goal setting and maintaining direction. (This is compatible with the Game of Work concept of not changing the rules in the middle of the game.) And certainly conducting such an exercise at least quarterly is not too frequent or too burdensome.

GETTING CLOSE TO THE TEAM

Tom Peters advised us to get close to the customer as one of the tenets of *In Search of Excellence*. Surely that includes staying close to the players on our team. One of the great exercises we have used in the consulting section of our work is to give employees the opportunity to give us the five changes they want to make in the company. We take the raw list and have it typed into a ballot. Then, using the same ranking technique made famous by the college team of the week (10 points, 9 points, 8 points, and so on), we have the group give us a ranked feelings report.

(You may obtain specific procedures for this exercise by sending a self-addressed stamped envelope with the words "Change Exercise" written on the outside to P.O. Box 1356, Park City, Utah 84060.)

The other process is called "Questions I wish someone else would ask the boss." There seems to be in every organization the need to be "in on things." This need is evidenced by the tremendous intelligence effort (rumor mills and old-fashioned gossip) that takes untold millions of labor hours to initiate, facilitate, and ultimately squelch or foster into full-blown wildfire. Why not recognize this obvious need and human force and harness it for the overall good of the organization? Let the need to know come into full force for the good of the goals and needs of the team. The most obvious motivation is the exchange system, where we all get what we want and create the win/win agreement that lasts and satisfies mutual needs.

One of the most proactive executives took this advice. In his national sporting goods manufacturing company, he conducts our Change Exercise each quarter with both employees and independent representatives. Then he responds to the most important items on the list. It takes only half a day of his time, and his answers usually come from the strategic plan or its tactical portion. The increase in focus is tremendous, and, perhaps more important, the entire company knows more of the answers they need. Beyond those benefits is the reduction in rumors and the general feeling his people have that they will get the answers to their questions and that the company is receptive to their ideas. There's an old song that says, "If you really listen, love is what you find." When you pay attention to this obvious source of authority, amazing things happen.

HOW TO GET MORE AUTHORITY

Want to get more authority yourself, as well as giving more to the people in your organization? Decide what you are going to *stop* doing. One way to approach this is to work on delegating or eliminating 5 percent of your tasks each quarter. That will give you a complete turnover in assignment every five years and keep you stimulated, challenged, and fresh. Another benefit is that when you start to delegate or eliminate tasks, you force yourself to focus on the most important and profitable activities, further improving your productivity. Perhaps most important, by delegating everything you can, you are giving your team continuous opportunities for growth. If your team can function without you, you are ready to be promoted—to receive additional authority. But if your team needs *you* to make the decisions *they* are being paid to make, how much authority do you have? Less authority than your team. An obvious conclusion, once you understand the principles upon which it is based. Now, what are you going to do about it?

8

COMPENSATION, THE OBVIOUS ISSUE

A re you underpaid? If you are like most people in the business world, you will answer with a resounding yes. But what is the appropriate relationship between your compensation and your contribution to your company? There are three possible variations once we decide that the relationship is direct and not inverse; compensation rises as the contribution rises and decreases as the contribution falls. They are:

1. Compensation > contribution.
2. Compensation = contribution.
3. Compensation < contribution.

COMPENSATION EXCEEDS CONTRIBUTION

When we talk about compensation exceeding contribution, we are not concerned with such temporary circumstances as hangovers, emotional concerns for the health of a loved one, or a half-hour morning coffee break that explores the merits of yesterday's ball game or shopping spree. No, rather we must examine the long-term effects of this possibility. It's called a deficit.

What we have in the United States government is a collective unwillingness to pay for what we want. We want more contribution from our government—more federal dollars to our state than the tax dollars we have donated from

our state. We want more social programs. We want everything, but we're not willing to pay for it, and that's where
the deficit comes from, because the compensation we desire, in terms of benefits taken out of government coffers, is
greater than the contributions we are willing to put into
them.

In the private sector, it is a shortfall or cash-flow problem to begin with and ultimately a cause of bankruptcy if it
is not checked. When you have unrealistic wage demands
or unrealistic owner takeout policies, the compensation
coming out is greater than the contribution going in. Consider all the athletes in baseball or basketball who are getting paid but aren't playing. They're currently getting about
$15,000,000—for nine guys. It's just insane.

During a strike at Kennecott Copper Company in Salt
Lake City, Utah, the company's management flew their strik-
ing employees down to the Biltmore Hotel in Phoenix, Arizona (at $150 per employee per night) to discuss union
rights. In my opinion, that was not very bright. They would
have obtained better results by taking them over to Consoli-
dated Freightways in Salt Lake City to sit in the parking lot
and look at all the empty trailers that aren't running anymore
because the teamsters insisted on all their benefits.

None of our organizations can long withstand withdrawals without deposits—not in our capital accounts, not
in our emotional bank accounts, and certainly not in our
productivity accounts.

Think about what happens when we try to withdraw
from the emotional bank account of someone close to us.
Divorce is often the result of one partner making too many
withdrawals—taking from the relationship more than he or
she is willing to put in. Eventually the compensation runs
out, and the relationship can no longer sustain the draw-
down of assets. Then the relationship collapses. I believe
you will agree that we cannot tolerate this condition to exist
for long in the business community.

Is this concept obvious? Let us see. In the next two days,
talk with a few associates (who do not report to you) and

bring up the topic. Find out what they believe is the proper relationship between compensation and contribution, and then ask them who on your team falls into each of the three categories.

COMPENSATION EQUALS CONTRIBUTION

The second relationship is where compensation equals contribution. Although at first this seems to be the correct relationship between the two, in the real world it cannot be. If it were so, the organization would pay out all of its revenues, retaining nothing for profit, growth, investment, equipment, and so on.

Even in interpersonal relationships, the concept of a 50/50 commitment is being replaced with the enlightened and enhanced idea of a 70/70 commitment, where those in the relationship give of themselves relative to each other's needs and not simply try to pay each other back for previous services rendered. Notice how wonderful a relationship with a pet can be, for example. The puppy that always wags its tail and the kitten that always cuddles bring great feelings of acceptance and warmth to the recipient of their affections.

This principle of putting in more than we take out is true, I believe, for all our important relationships, and the principle works for both people in a relationship, whether we are talking about a husband and wife, a coach and a player, or an employer and an employee. An employee needs to contribute to the company, but he or she also needs to receive fair compensation for doing so.

We have heard a great deal lately about the need for entrepreneurship and intrapreneurship. It is my considered observation that you cannot get entrepreneurial performance with communal compensation. As long as our compensation programs are devised to minimize individual differences, we will continue to suffer losses in productivity. Is there a management challenge in having to determine a scorekeeping system that compensates people on the basis of their contribution? You bet there is! But those who are unwilling to take up that challenge will never manage superbowl champions. Coaches who are unwilling to create feedback systems for their players that show them how to be successful just before the official score is turned in will never have great official scores.

Let me make a point at this juncture for the skeptics who say, "You can't expect people to work for direct compensation. You can't find people who are willing to place their family's security at risk. People want guarantees. People want to be paid just for showing up." Well, let's get something straight: all compensation is direct, whether it's bargained for or modified through the structured regime of salary administration. The truth is that any time compensation is not proportionate to the contribution (and therefore direct), the relationship, whether in business, marriage, or family, is on the threshold of collapse.

However, you cannot have pure *equality* in a relationship because equal is not always equitable. We further complicate things by the inappropriate assumption that people in the same position must receive the same compensation. We need to keep the differential in the compensation at least as wide as the performance of the players. There is no equality or equity in a system that allows only 8 percent variation in compensation when there is clearly 20 percent or more variation in the profitability and productivity of the players.

CONTRIBUTION IS GREATER THAN COMPENSATION

The obvious conclusion we must draw is that in a healthy organization or relationship, contribution from each individual and the group as a whole must exceed compensation. In other words, everybody is going to be underpaid. That's not a great breakthrough in managerial thinking, but what is a breakthrough is recognizing that is the only way it can be. So if you're sitting in an organization saying, "I'm underpaid," you have to realize that is just part of life. But associated with that is the fact that you can continue to raise your contribution to the organization and watch your compensation rise with it. Of course, you'll still be underpaid. But it's good to see that as a healthy thing and not make yourself and others miserable by whining and moaning about it.

This principle is also complicated by the diverse nature of measurement on the two sides of the equation. Compensation tends to be rather specific. Most people can tell you to the penny how much they are paid. They may also say that money is not the most important motivator in their job, but they can tell you how much they receive on an hourly, daily, weekly, monthly, and annual basis. They know!

Also, your company undoubtedly has someone whose job is to make sure that paychecks are accurate each payday, and departments of city, state, and federal governments monitor and are committed to the preservation of workers' rights and the correctness of the compensation side of the arrangement. And that is without adding the enforcement of a collective bargaining agreement!

We even do annual surveys to help us with salary administration, all in the name of a fair day's wage. Decades of enlightenment on the part of American society have effectively eliminated the sweatshop environment for all but the entrepreneurial few, and, don't forget, they choose to work that way! But the problem today is still, as Frederick Taylor said it was in 1892 (yes, 1892!) that the toughest task management has is to define what constitutes a fair day's job.

And we can't forget that it is a job! We have dedicated so much energy to the easiest side of the equation, compensation, that we have given insufficient thought to the part that pays off, contribution. And we seem to have created this thought in the minds of our workers: "If you give me more compensation, I'll give you more of the undefined contribution." That has been so much a part of our culture, both with and without collective bargaining, that we have priced ourselves out of many of the very industries that formed the foundation of American leadership in the world's economy—autos, steel, extractive minerals, heavy equipment, and consumer electronics are some that immediately come to mind. This gap has been caused by the inequity in the measurement system. And what has happened is that we have masked the obvious. We cannot have the Chilean copper miner taking more tonnage per hour out of the mine than the American counterpart and then compound the problem with artificially high negotiated labor rates that contribute to a non-competitive situation in the world market. Compensation cannot exceed contribution for very long.

I once knew an executive vice-president of a personal services firm who was constantly asking for more authority, a bigger company car, and other perks. He also wanted increased staffing and an additional personal secretary. Interestingly enough, his requests came during a period when productivity and profitability were down, almost always a mistake. While his monetary compensation was directly tied to sales, his indirect compensation kept growing, even though his contribution to the company was in decline.

Another problem began cropping up as well, his attitude. He began blaming his shortfall in contribution on everything from the state of the economy, to the quality of the salespeople being recruited (for whom he was directly responsible), to the way the accounting department handled his expense account. After several months of this nonsense, the company's majority stockholder decided he could no longer accept the inequity in the contribution/compensation formula and dissolved the firm.

That's the kind of thing that happens when compensation exceeds contribution. It never works. So what is required is to acknowledge the obvious principle that we must:

1. Define the contribution currently being delivered.

2. Increase that contribution to necessary levels to maintain and enhance the competitive level of the organization.

3. Expect that an increase in compensation will assuredly follow as day follows night.

The law of the harvest says we must sow *before* we can reap, and that is true in every area of life. Great companies, like great spouses and great players and great coaches, understand this principle and follow it. They're always asking themselves, "What else can I put into this relationship?" If I'm half bright at all, I'll always be asking myself, relative to my kids, my friends, or my business partners, "What else can I do for them?" I'll be asking myself, "What else can I do tonight for my spouse? What am I willing to do to enhance our relationship?" That gets me on the offensive. That makes me proactive. I am acting on life rather than reacting to it. Stephen R. Covey, one of the great management consultants and thinkers of our time, lists proactivity as one of the seven habits of highly effective people. (See his book *The Seven Habits of Highly Effective People* [New York: Simon & Schuster, 1989].) And proactivity is merely asking and responding to such questions as: "How can I build my contribution?" "How can I rearrange my schedule to get more done?" "How can I work smarter so that I can bring about more of the things I want to have happen in my life and the lives of others?"

A good example of someone whose contribution was greater than his compensation is Lee Iacocca, who worked for $1.00 a year in salary until Chrysler could pay back the federally guaranteed loan that kept them afloat through perilous times. Of course, he was criticized for later cashing in $12 million worth of stock options and grants. But perhaps his ability to do so also has something to do with his unarguably enormous contribution to his company.

Another example: In the early 1980s, the owner of the Philadelphia 76'ers hired Moses Malone as a free agent. Malone was a truly great player, and there was much speculation about the increased revenues he would bring to the ball club, in everything from ticket sales to beer sales to parking. Malone was paid $2.2 million that first season, during which he helped pick up the NBA title for the team and added approximately $13 million to the bottom line. When the 76'ers faced the Los Angeles Lakers in the final series,

Kareem Abdul-Jabar was making noises about how he deserved to be paid more than Malone for his great talent. Then Malone and the 76'ers beat the Lakers in four straight games. Kareem quietly settled for $1.25 million a year in his contract renewal. While inequities sometimes occur, in the long run the marketplace tends to reward us in proportion to our ability to overcontribute.

We also need to look at the ways we can overcontribute in our personal lives. My wife, Carla, and I have a regular program to get away from the humdrum of everyday life and renew our relationship. We were in Hawaii for twelve days for our fifteenth anniversary. She went to Boston with me the last time I spoke there. She and our children came to San Diego when I had a presentation there. The point is that our kids were saying, "Wow! We're going on a cruise with Dad." Of course, I had to speak for four hours, so it wasn't a pleasure trip. But the idea is that we always need to be asking ourselves, "How do I put more in? How can I give more to my spouse? How can I work more effectively with my business partner? How can I better serve my customers? What vast improvements can I make in what I do for other people? What else can I do? What's the next thing I can do?" This is the law of the harvest: "As ye sow, so shall ye reap." "Cast your bread upon the waters, and after many days it will return to you."

Very few people spend a lot of time thinking about how much they can give. But the people we most look up to, people like Mother Theresa, Albert Schweitzer, Martin Luther King, Mahatma Gandhi, and Jesus of Nazareth, do. In fact, those kind of people probably don't spend *any* time thinking about what they are going to get back. They are worried only about putting in everything they've got.

Life usually seems to reward our whole-hearted efforts many times over. We give out, and life gives back. It's like the law of buoyancy. If you throw a cork up in the air over a bowl of water, gravity brings the cork down and temporarily overcomes buoyancy, as the cork sinks a little bit at the end of its fall. But if you push the cork into the water and then let go, its buoyancy as overcomes gravity temporarily, shooting the cork a little way into the air. Then the cork settles back down again. The point is, life tends to give more when you give more. The principle works with people, too: If you dedicate yourself to overcontributing, the other person in the deal will break his or her back to keep things even.

As Ralph Waldo Emerson wrote in his essay "Compensation": "The nature and soul of things takes on itself the guaranty of the fulfilment of every contract, so that honest service cannot come to loss. If you serve an ungrateful master, serve him the more. Put God in your debt. Every stroke shall be repaid." (In *Essays by Ralph Waldo Emerson* [New York: Thomas Y. Crowell Company, 1926; reprinted in Perennial Library edition by Harper & Row], p.86.)

I believe this is just as much a law of nature as the fact that air traveling over a curved plane, such as the wing of a jet, will lift that plane into the air, something I always marvel at, especially when I'm sitting in a sixty-ton 747 thirty thousand feet over the ocean. It seems impossible, but it holds true every time.

We see the law of the harvest at work very clearly in the areas of customer service and productivity delivery, and we must constantly be working on how to better serve our customers. This is especially true if we in American business are to remain competitive in the areas we yet dominate (such as computer software, innovation, and recreation) and to regain an appropriate share in other areas (such as automobiles and consumer electronics). Our ignoring of the obvious has led to second-class status for our nation and our economy.

My analysis in this chapter may appear naive or simplistic, but I have worked thousands of hours in many different industries and even non-profit organizations, and I can assure you that the approach I am advocating works. When the team makes the commitment to serve ahead of the expected reward, the realized reward always exceeds the players' expectations. This leap of faith is more than an

obvious principle of good business. It transcends our interpersonal relationships and affects even the relationships we
form with our environment.

One intriguing factor is the existence of the law of natural balance in relationship to the law of overcontributing.
Most of us believe we are currently overcontributing. Ask
almost anyone you know, and I believe that person will try
to tell you that he or she is underpaid. No one is going to
confess that he or she is undercontributing. So we have
agreed on the obvious; now we simply need to get over the
frustration we feel about the situation and realize that is the
way it must be for growth and progress. Of course we are
underpaid! And aren't we glad about our opportunities to
continue to overcontribute and then receive the correct reward? How much better it is to be waiting for the reward
we have rightfully earned than to be behind and in fear of
the consequences of our actions. I believe so. Draw your
own conclusions; then determine now to act.

9

THE POWER OF PRINCIPLES

On his twenty-eighth birthday, a successful friend of mine was approached by his father, who told him, "Jim, I want to retire. I'm ready for other, more pleasurable activities, and I'd like you to take over our family business. A ship can have only one captain, and you are mature and experienced enough to be that captain." The son had known that one day he would head the company, but the timing of the transfer of leadership came as a surprise.

"However," the father said, "there are four principles I expect you to follow in running the company. As long as you follow those principles, you can do anything you want. But if at any time you don't follow them, I'll be back in a heartbeat. That's how important those principles are."

Now, many years later, the son still guides the company with those same four principles. He has been faithful to them since taking over, and he has preached them to his employees and friends. They have brought him great success.

Principle number one is to astonish the customer, not just to satisfy the customer in any of the more common or haphazard ways. The company must vastly exceed the customer's expectations.

The second principle is to be debt free. The father explained that those who need to borrow money frequently are doing something wrong. In fact, they are probably losing money or expanding the company too quickly. Internally financed growth is better than externally financed growth. For example, factoring receivables, usually at rates greater than profit margins, disguises other problems that must be fixed before the company can grow properly.

The third principle is to make the company feel like a home, not just a home for the members of management but for all of the employees and their families. Competitive compensation and benefit packages are expected in today's market. But beyond these are the "creature comforts," the human side. You know when you've created a home environment because your employees demonstrate their happiness in a variety of productive and creative ways. They have more respect for the company's assets. They care more for the products and services. And they stretch their efforts and abilities a little more.

The fourth principle is to make a profit. This principle may sound obvious, but it's amazing how many executives forget this most basic of principles and do things, even well-meaning things, that keep their company from being profitable. Making a profit means having a long-term perspective of customers' needs, sales growth, and expense control. It means understanding the need to spend a dime in order to make a dollar. It means having a long-range and realistic perspective of who you are and what your company really does. Companies need guiding principles, no less than three and no more than five. What are yours? If your company doesn't have any, what principles do you think they should adopt?

THE HAND-HOLDS OF LIFE

A principle is a concept or belief that can stand the test of time. It has an application beyond today, beyond what you can see at the moment. It's something you can trust and believe in. Principles are the hand-holds of life, offering us stability and enabling us to keep focused on the values that drive success.

Principles are obvious because they usually stare us in the face, like flashing beacon lights, making them difficult to ignore. For some reason, principles remain the same; they are constant. Nevertheless, some people become very good at ignoring the principles that would otherwise make them successful. Some people have a talent for looking directly at the obvious principles that could bring them success and then claiming they don't exist.

I've watched many successful people use basic or guiding principles to overcome obstacles and achieve success. I've also observed how ignoring obvious principles can bring failure. What are the guiding principles in your life and in your company? How can you identify them? How do you follow them?

PROVEN PRINCIPLES FOR SUCCESS

The spectacular success of the Disney organization can only be attributed to Walt Disney himself. He was the driving force who created the impetus that drove success. The Disney organization prospered by sticking to basic principles that Walt himself developed and preached to his associates. He once called them his "secrets" and another time referred to them as "five ways to make dreams come true." They are the guiding principles of the Disney philosophy, and they helped Walt build one of the best organizations in the history of business.

1. *Think tomorrow.* Walt Disney believed that what you do today must make tomorrow pay off. If your actions today don't support success for tomorrow, you're headed in the wrong direction. Too much thinking and acting for today can distort your vision of what is possible tomorrow. Walt was a true visionary leader because he didn't let today's activities and problems get in the way of effectively planning for tomorrow.

2. *Free the imagination.* Walt Disney believed that people can accomplish far more than they normally achieve. The limiting factor of most people, he explained, is their inability to use their imagination. By thinking outside the usual, normal, or expected, wonderful things can happen. Disney's creations are a prime example of freeing the imagination. He created an organizational culture where illustrators, writers, and designers could create the unexpected.

3. *Strive for quality.* In 1938 Walt refused to release an animated film because he felt that it lacked enduring quality. After six months of revisions on the concept, Pinocchio was released and became a classic. Walt's insistence on quality changed a good film into a great film that has endured for over half a century.

4. *Have "stick-to-it-ivity."* Walt once told a magazine writer that one of his secrets of success was his fortitude and his "stick-to-it-ivity." He made up the word to describe himself and later used the same word in a song sung by an owl in *So Dear to My Heart* (1940). Too many people quit after the first, second, third, or fourth failure. Walt's perseverance and refusal to quit in the face of adversity is a testament to his personal character and determination.

5. *Have fun.* "The way to make things work is not to worry," Walt once said. "Get interested in [an] idea that looks fun [and make it work]." The ability to laugh is rare in some organizations. Too often, stress and tension get in the way of creative and productive thinking. If Walt were alive today, he would say to many of us, "Lighten up!"

Walt even gave Mickey Mouse guiding principles to live by. He described Mickey's philosophy of life as having three attributes. First, Mickey has a perpetual smile. Second, he is optimistic. And third, he has a "can do" spirit. Those characteristics, or guiding principles, wouldn't be bad for any of us, or our organizations, today.

Ray Noorda, the leader who built Novell, Inc., into a household name in the computer industry, credits his success to five two-word principles:

- Work hard
- Cash fast
- Play some
- Pray lots
- Pure luck

When you think about his five principles, it's difficult to disagree with them. Working hard, paying attention to cash flow, not forgetting to unwind and play, giving credit to a supreme being, and then taking advantage of lucky or fortunate opportunities all make sense.

Tom Peters, in his book *In Search of Excellence* (New York: Harper and Row, 1982), defines and examines the outstanding characteristics of excellent companies. These could easily be adapted as basic principles in running a business. The characteristics are:

- bias for action
- closeness to the customer
- autonomy and entrepreneurship
- productivity through people
- hands-on, value-driven
- stick to the knitting
- simple form, lean staff
- simultaneous loose-tight properties

If you don't know what these mean, I strongly suggest that you read this masterwork of modern management.

Benjamin Franklin put great stock in identifying and following basic principles, and he penned many of them as proverbs. Most of these he published under the pen name of Richard Saunders in the famous *Poor Richard's Almanac*. Highly popular with the American colonists in the 1700s, they are still meaningful today:

- "No man e'er was glorious, who was not laborious."
- "To be humble to Superiors is Duty, to Equals Courtesy, to Inferiors Nobleness."
- "Diligence is the Mother of Good Luck."
- "Beware of little Expenses, a small leak will sink a great ship."
- "No gains without pains."

- "Being ignorant is not so much a Shame, as being unwilling to learn."
- "Creditors have better memories that debtors."

Would you like to know my basic principles? Here they are:

- Compete against yourself.
- Associate with the best.
- See more sunrises and fewer midnights.

Principles for a Day

An easy way to experiment with new principles in your life is to try one on for a day. It isn't necessary to commit to a new set of principles overnight; you can adopt one or two principles for a day at a time. Consider, for example, adopting one these basic principles:

- Be optimistic to your co-workers.
- Hand out more smiles.
- Compliment more.
- Laugh more.
- Look for the good in yourself.
- Look for the good in others.
- Understand others' points of view before you tell them yours.
- Spend time with someone who needs your attention.
- Tell others that you appreciate their efforts.
- Encourage others to recommend solutions.
- Forgive others who have offended you.
- Tell someone that you value their judgment.
- Tell someone that you respect their opinion.
- Give someone an opportunity to do something new.
- Surprise someone with your attention.

After you have identified several obvious principles that work for you and your organization, don't keep them to yourself; pass them on. Post them on the wall. List them at the bottom of memos. Distribute them with your mission statement. Publish them in the company newsletter. Talk about them in your annual speech at the company banquet.

Cicero, the great Roman orator and senator, gave many speeches on many subjects, but at the end of each speech he always said the same thing: "Carthage must be destroyed." It wasn't long before this principle that he preached with such persistence became reality, and the city was reduced to rubble.

Get your principles out into your company. When you do, people pick them up and begin moving in a unified direction—the direction that you, the captain of the ship, have set. When you don't, people still work according to principles—those they have picked up from everyplace else they have ever worked. Is that what you want? Make your principles crystal clear. The distillation and distribution of your most important values will make an enormous difference in your business and in your life.

DIRECTING
THE
OBVIOUS

10

MOTIVATION, THE OBVIOUS MYSTERY

My friend Rick, when he was fourteen years old, worked as a stock boy in a shoe store for seventy-five cents an hour. It was a small store, with a sales floor out front, a tiny back room, and a stock room where last season's unsold shoes were kept. Twice a year, all of the stock had to be rearranged to accommodate the change in summer and winter shoe styles. That meant moving the new shoes from the back room to the sales floor, the old shoes from the sales floor to the stock room, and, finally, last year's remaining shoes from the stock room to the sales floor—a big job, especially considering that the stock room was three stories above the sales floor and the only way up was to take the stairs. In April, a huge shipment of spring and summer shoes came in, and it was time for the big event.

The manager of the shoe store, whose name was Ralph, preferred to be addressed as Mister R. And he was—at least to his face. Behind his back, however, the stockers called him "RRRRalph," trying to see who could roll the most gutteral R. As you may have surmised, Ralph was not well liked. With the new shipment of shoes, the back room was so full of boxes that the employees couldn't even get to the restooms. So Ralph told two stockers—Rick and Donnie—to come in at four o'clock the next morning—a Saturday—and make the big switch. "It's an eight-hour job," he told them, which meant it was really a ten-hour job but he would pay them for eight—a trick he had pulled before. Now you know why they called him "RRRRalph."

At the appointed hour, they were there, and the work was not fun. But after an hour of trudging up and down the three flights of stairs with boxes full of shoes, Donnie told Rick, "Bet I can make the circuit faster than you," and the race was on! Rick timed him as he grabbed boxes from the back room and ran them to the sales floor, grabbed more boxes from the sales floor and ran them upstairs, grabbed shoes from upstairs and ran them to the sales floor, and finally rushed back to the back room. "Nice job," Rick said. "Ninety seconds." Then he was off, with Donnie doing the timing. He made it back in a few seconds less than ninety. And on they went for several hours (when you're fourteen years old you can do that), trying to set what they called the World Land Speed Record. They tried giving each other five-second head starts to see if they could catch up with each other. They practiced taking the landings in only two steps, with the goal being not to drop any boxes. By eight-thirty, half an hour before the store was to open, 90 percent of the job was done.

The two exhausted competitors sat down for a well-deserved break in the back room, sweat pouring down their foreheads and their legs trembling from all that exertion. As they rubbed their cold soda bottles over their faces, they began talking about what Ralph would say when he saw the job they had done. Maybe he would let them go home early. Maybe he would raise them to eighty cents an hour. Maybe he would even give them a promotion! At the very least, he would surely be impressed by the astonishing job they had done and give them a kind word, which in itself would make the whole year worthwhile.

Right about then, in walked Ralph. Did he notice the nearly empty back room? Did he notice the clear access to the restrooms? No. But he did notice the two stock boys taking a break on his time. And this is what he said: "Do I pay you lazy [expletive] for moving freight, or do I pay you for sitting on your fat [expletive]?"

As it turned out, Ralph's original estimate was right: it was an eight-hour job. The last 10 percent of the work took the remaining three and a half hours.

Perhaps you once worked for Ralph (only his name may have been George or Shirley)—someone whose concept of motivation was to beat people up emotionally. Unfortunately, there are too many Ralphs in the world. Why? I believe that abuse, in businesses as well as in families, is passed on from generation to generation, and the sweat shop mentality is still with us today. But now is the time to break the link and take a more enlightened—not to mention effective—approach to motivating our players.

I believe that motivation is the most misunderstood concept in all of human relations. If you, as a manager, are not concerned about the motivation of your people each day, then you are not managing your most important asset.

THE MOTIVATION OF EXTRINSIC VALUE

How do we motivate others (and ourselves)? First we have to understand that motivation is an exchange system. You give me what I want, and I give you what you want. As a friend of mine is fond of saying, "There ain't no sacrifice."

Let me give you an example. Suppose we are sitting across the table from each other, and I have in my hand a hundred-dollar bill, a fifty, and a twenty. You have a five-dollar bill. Will you give it to me?

"For what?" you naturally ask. But I'm not willing to tell you yet. So I ask again, "Will you give me the five?"

If you say yes, there's probably a very good reason. Maybe we've had some dealings in the past, so you feel you can trust me. Also, you've probably worked with me enough to think that if you give me the five, you'll get a five-dollar idea. Or you may think that you'll get a twenty back, in money or in ideas. In that case, giving me the five isn't a sacrifice—it's an investment.

Now, if you don't know me and I ask for the five, you may put it out on the table, but you'll probably keep your hand on it, waiting to see what you'll get in return. If you just give me the five without hope for a greater return, that's sacrifice, a donation. You might do it once, but will you continue to do it? Will you continue to give me the five without receiving something in exchange? I once had a car that kept requiring small repairs—fifty dollars here, fifty dollars there. Each time I hoped it would be the last fifty dollars. And one day it was, because I *said* it was the last fifty dollars. And eventually that's the point you will get to in our relationship if I never give you anything in return for all those fives. Even if you trust me, at some point you're going to say, "That's enough. It's over."

All of this may seem self-evident, but think about this example in relation to your business, and you'll begin to understand the fundamental principles of how to motivate people. Obviously they're not going to sacrifice—at least not for very long. But what if you offer them a twenty for their five? Will they take it? Of course they will. What if you offer them the fifty if they'll give you the twenty? They'll take it every time. And will they give you the fifty in return for the hundred? You'd better believe it. So motivation is simply an exchange system. I'm going to expend my energy, my time, my talent, and my caring for what I perceive as a greater benefit.

Seems obvious. But if it's obvious, why don't we behave as if we believe it? Why are there Ralphs in the world? The Ralph mentality began in the 1920s, when managers assumed that workers had no other option but to do as they were told. And that kind of motivation works—as long as fear is present and there really is no other place to go. A manager might say, "You work your tail off and I have a dollar for you." But if another manager across the street said, "Work hard, work straight, work honest, and I'll give you two dollars," where would you go? And you'd probably go for one dollar and some kindness and appreciation.

If motivation is that simple, why have we spent the past thirty years expending an ever-larger percentage of our compensation program paying people *not* to go to work?

Just think about all the benefits and incentives to stay away. In some companies, if you work hard, you don't have to work as long. You've finished the project and tolerated my management style, so you get next week off. In some organizations, you can actually make more money by getting hurt and staying on Workman's Compensation. Unemployment benefits used to run up to twenty-six weeks. After that you had to get back to work because you wouldn't be paid anymore for staying home. The Carter administration's answer to the problem was to extend benefits for another twenty-six weeks—a whole year altogether. No wonder 8 percent of the population was unemployed during that time! Carter actually aggravated the problem he was trying to solve. Of course it doesn't make sense. But do we do any better in our businesses? We invest millions of dollars in early retirement programs, sick leave, insurance premiums, and income continuation—all so that people will stay away. We spend a thousand times more encouraging nonproductivity than we ever do training our managers to make the work environment more acceptable.

Where are we doing a great job of providing motivation to work? In profit-sharing plans, prepaid child care, matching-fund savings plans, and many others. All are important in getting people to make a greater contribution to the company.

What motivates people? Why are people motivated to buy the Lexus, for example? They buy it because of the cost-benefit ratio when compared to other cars. Once again, it's an exchange value. I can buy a Lexus for $45,000 as opposed to $85,000 for the German equivalent, and the Lexus has more features—lots more. But the formula is not all economic. Many people still buy that German alternative, and depending on the value of our currency against the mark, the prices may be even closer. Porsches sell at a premium compared to vehicles of similar horsepower and performance, but there is still something intangible about *owning*, not just *driving* the Porsche. Exchange value—the willingness to exchange one thing for another.

The Motivation of Intrinsic Value

Consider the Mary Kay pink Cadillac. Who do you think pays for it? The woman driving it. To get the car, she accepts considerably less commission than she would be paid if she didn't take the car. And Mary Kay corporate headquarters doesn't give her the choice of a cash equivalent. When she reaches a certain distribution level, she gets a pink Cadillac. She also pays taxes on it, whether she wants it or not and whether she likes the color or not. Now let me ask you a question: Across the board, how many people do you know who would *buy* a pink Cadillac? None. So what's the attraction for Mary Kay distributors? They're getting more than a Cadillac. They're getting the intrinsic value of a membership in an elite group of Mary Kay distributors, and that's what motivates them to achieve that level of production.

Another example: Do you like the color of a Century 21 real estate agent's blazer—that mustard gold? Would you have a coat like that in your closet? Would you wear it to the corporate dinner? Would you wear it anywhere? No. But that coat isn't just a coat. It represents something: leadership, teamwork, better listings, and customer recognition and confidence—all important exchange factors in the mind of the real estate agent.

Consider the Rolex watch, which sells for around $15,000. Why would anyone buy one? Because it keeps good time? Nope. A $10 plastic import from Korea does just as good a job. But if you pick up a copy of *Sports Illustrated*, you'll almost always see an expensive, full-color, full-page ad for Rolex watches. Even with the high cost of a Rolex, do you realize how many watches they've got to sell each month just to cover the cost of the ads? How many people do you know who wear a Rolex? How many people do you know who bought one last month? I can't think of anybody. But somebody must have! And you can bet they didn't do it so they'd have an accurate timepiece.

The point is, an exchange value can be intrinsic (inner)

as well as extrinsic (outer)—and often the intrinsic value is more important than the extrinsic. The value is in the eye of the beholder. Michael Jordan gets $3 million a year to wear Nikes. Why? Well, there's a lot of intrinsic value there. Michael signs with Nike rather than Adida or Asics or Avia because, in his own mind, the exchange value is greater—Nike is a more prestigious shoe. In return, Nike pays Michael because of what the endorsement does for them in the number of Air Jordans they sell—it's nice to be associated with a hero. The kids who buy the Air Jordans perceive the social value of the more expensive shoe, and the parents who pay for it have similar motivation—it says something about the level of their success.

Actually, everything we work for, including money, has intrinsic as well as extrinsic value; the real exchange value exists only in the mind. Business writer Robert J. Ringer makes this point in his book *Looking Out for Number One*. According to Ringer, there is no selflessness; everything we do is for the exchange value of something better. Take the idea of raising money for Jerry's Kids, for example. The employees in a large corporation donate $21 million out of their pockets for the telethon. The CEO gets to appear on national TV and hand over the check, and everybody says, "How wonderful!" And it is wonderful. Let's just not kid ourselves into believing that they're not getting anything out of it.

While there are undoubtedly exceptions, many anonymous donations are made by people who tell themselves, "I'm better than all those glory grabbers." A good example is millionaire Sam Jex. He'll give out $1 million to a worthy cause as long as the people will keep quiet about where they got the money. Then he'll turn around in the same year and give another $1 million to put up a university building—as long as his name goes on the building. To me, it doesn't make sense. But it makes sense to Sam! And if you want to get Sam's million, you've got to convince him that the cause is right—relative to him.

The point is that different people are motivated for

different reasons—different strokes for different folks—and that's a very powerful thing to know. What intrinsic values motivate your players? If you don't know, maybe it's time to ask, and then to begin consciously using those values to provide greater motivation in the workplace.

THE MOTIVATION OF PURPOSE

Often, people are motivated because it allows them to be part of a higher purpose. The story is told of an old man who stopped to watch the bricklayers at a construction site. "What are you doing?" he asked one of the workers. "I'm laying brick," the laborer said, "and I'll sure be glad when this job is over with."

The old man went on to another worker. "What are you doing," he asked. "I'm just finishing this wall," the bricklayer said. "Thank goodness it's nearly quitting time."

As he was leaving the construction site, the old man asked a third bricklayer, "What are you doing?" The bricklayer put down his trowel and unrolled a blueprint. "I'm building this cathedral," he said. "I'm building a house of God. Isn't it beautiful?"

The third bricklayer had related his toilsome job to the overall construction process, and, more important, he had come to appreciate the purpose of the project on which he was working. He understood and was motivated by a higher purpose—an exchange value well worth working for.

What are your cathedrals? What is the vision—the higher purpose—you must help your team to see?

THE MOTIVATION OF RECREATION

At the beginning of this chapter, we discussed two stock boys who were motivated to do an extraordinary job—not by their obnoxious boss, Ralph, but because they were trying to beat each other's record. That's what I call the motivation of recreation, and it is central to the idea of the Game of Work.

I saw the motivation of recreation at work when a large regional foods distributor asked us to participate with their warehouse staff in reducing their shrink. The story has an interesting side note that I had not expected. In the second session with the company, we talked about the joy of measurement and the benefit of daily feedback. One of the associates in the program became so enthusiastic about the idea that he went right out and created a scorekeeping system so the forklift drivers in the warehouse could measure their productivity. The job of the forklift operators is to let down full pallets of groceries, from high cube storage to eye-level selection racks, so order pickers can get at the merchandise. It's a premium job, a bid job, and a job for seniority, but it's not a job where you find a great deal of first-year enthusiasm or young workers trying to make their mark.

I have always maintained that we must allow people to *choose* to compete, and that scorecards that force competition among people tend to have a negative effect. Shows you how wrong the experts can be. These people took their new scorecard, wrote down their scores, and then taped them up on the wall for all to see. In seventy-two hours, three shifts later, they had moved from 11.75 let-downs per hour to 16 per hour, about a 33 percent improvement in productivity.

Now, we pay forklift operators by the hour, which doesn't really motivate the behavior we want repeated—doing the let-downs. If one of the key functions of feedback is to motivate the behavior we want repeated, then the first responsibility of managers is to determine what they want. Having made that determination, they are much more capable of deciding how to pay for it. Far too often, we have ignored what it is we want done. We pay people by the hour, which is basically just paying people for attendance, and then we complain about the fact that they are unmotivated. Obviously we want more pallet let-downs per shift; obviously we want a higher velocity of merchandise turning through the warehouse. In this case, once we said so through a simple, single-page scorekeeping system, we got that 33 percent increase in productivity.

Why does such improvement occur? Well, paying for it helps, but that is not the primary factor. It occurs because when we keep score, our work is no longer just a job. It is a way to get ahead, to be better than we used to be, and to enjoy our work. People naturally want to improve, if we give them the chance to do so and recognition when they do. And that may be the most important key to understanding the obvious mystery of motivation.

11

SELF-IMAGE, THE OBVIOUS FOUNDATION

Most of my life, I have loved sleek, shiny Corvettes—red ones, blue ones—or how about a silver one? Beautiful. While I was in college, I used to get into my fifteen-year-old green four-door Plymouth and drive down to the local Chevrolet dealership, where I would drool over the latest model of Corvette. Someday, I vowed, as soon as I could afford one, I would have that 'Vette.

After I entered the workforce, the years began to roll by. Eventually twelve of them had rolled by, and I still didn't have the car. I was beginning to wonder if I ever would. In the fall of 1974, I bought a Jeep—the payments were within my reach.

One fine day a couple of years later, just for fun, I went down to the lot and found a 1972 Corvette—the car of my dreams. It was a platinum metallic beauty with a dark-brown leather interior. I knew I couldn't afford it, but the dealer, like all who sell cars for a living, still seemed eager to talk to me. This time, maybe because I realized I had nothing to lose, I decided to listen. We looked up the trade-in value of my Jeep and figured out the whole deal on paper. To my immense surprise, the payment on the Corvette was just eight dollars more per month than what I had been paying on the Jeep. I could have my Corvette!

Then I realized what I had done. For years I had unnecessarily put off my dream because I had thought it was out of the question. I just had not believed that I, Chuck Coonradt, could swing it, and I had been too scared to find out whether I could or not. Now, almost by accident, I had found out that I could. I learned a great lesson that day about self-image and self-confidence.

YOUR SELF-IMAGE

Do you believe in yourself? Do you believe you can achieve your goals? Do you see yourself as a whopping success, as an underachiever, or, like most people, as doing pretty well some of the time and needing some improvement at other times? Most people would agree that a healthy self-image is a cornerstone of success and growth in any pursuit. The obvious question is how to develop that healthier self-image in ourselves and in those with whom we work.

What is the basis for self-image? Self-image is based upon what you know and can prove about yourself. The most obvious examples are age, sex, financial status, and other physical characteristics. But we also have fairly specific mental images of our mental and emotional characteristics. Do you know people who, in spite of irrefutable financial success, demean their accomplishments with a phrase like "Not bad for a kid who didn't get out of the eighth grade"? That is the real self-image coming through. Unfortunately, people often describe themselves in negative terms, and this undoubtedly influences their behavior and their level of accomplishment.

The only way I can improve how I feel about myself is to change what I know about my performance—and not just what I know, but what I can prove. A former associate and good friend, Jack Kelley, says, "We'll take anybody's word for our failures, but we demand proof positive for our successes." He is right, and if we are going to build a winning team, we need to acknowledge that wisdom and make it work for us.

People will do only what they believe they can do. As leaders and managers, we can temporarily inspire improved performance. But to create permanent change, we must raise the belief and subsequently the self-confidence and self-image of the players.

How would you like to have the secret of building your *own* self-image? Sound great? It's obvious.

Suppose you are looking at an X-ray of yourself, but at an emotional X-ray, not the kind that comes from the radiology lab. Look right down through the top of your head into the core of yourself. Right in the middle is your self-image or your self-concept. Now, what makes up that self-image? Your experiences, knowledge, feelings, and so on. But more important, it's based on what you know and can prove about yourself.

is what you *know*
and can *prove* about yourself

Let's go down to the bowling alley, where I can demonstrate this principle. Imagine that you are a 155 bowler; in other words, your *average* score is 155. Sometimes you get a little above that; sometimes you get a little below it. But 155 is your average. Is that part of what you know and can prove? Sure. You just take the score sheets from your past games and figure it up. Now, I'm going to bet you a thousand dollars, even money, that you can't bowl 165 in one out of five lines. Would you take that bet? If you're like many people, you would, because even though it's a stretch, it's fairly close to what you know you can do. Also, you now have five chances to do it, with a thousand-dollar payoff if you succeed. The 165 is in an area we call your self-confidence, which is what you *think* you know about yourself. If you look at the emotional X-ray of yourself, it is the circle around the core of your self-image. It is based on your self-image, and it is the part of you that allows you to stretch beyond what you currently know about yourself in order to try something new, in order to grow.

Would you take the bet at 170? How about 175? Do you now notice a difference in the difficulty of making the decision? Probably. Why? Because the consequences of the decision are becoming more likely to be negative. So now we can summarize with four points about self-confidence:

1. Your self-confidence is based on your self-image—what you know and can prove about yourself.

2. Self-confidence is measurable and finite—you have limits to how far you will go. A score of 200 is probably out of the question, for example.

3. Your self-image and self-confidence are situational.

4. Your self-image and self-confidence are developable and expandable.

But will you take the bet at 200 if I give you odds of 100 to 1? Same circumstances: one out of five games. If you lose, you still have to pay me $1,000, but if you win, you get $100,000. Well? Maybe you wouldn't, because you probably can't bowl that well even if you get lucky, and you don't want to lose the thousand dollars. In other words, even though the prize would be great if you won, the penalty for losing is so *likely* to occur that you wouldn't take the bet.

But would you take the bet at 200 if you only had to put up ten bucks? To win $100,000? Of course. Why? Because the consequences of losing are so low that you would gladly take the shot at winning the $100,000. After all, you might get *really* lucky. This also explains why so many people will spend the cost of a first-class stamp to mail their entry to the Publisher's Clearinghouse Sweepstakes. They know the chances of winning are next to nothing. But, on the other hand, it doesn't cost much to enter. And there *is* a chance they might win, however small.

So here's the lesson: *When your goals are beyond your self-confidence, you are more concerned and focused on what you have to lose than on what you have to gain.* As a result, the "protect-what-I-have" part of you says you won't stretch.

Self-confidence and self-image are situational. And both self-confidence and self-image are expandable; otherwise, we wouldn't believe in self-improvement. The problem is that most people have goals that are beyond their self-confidence, so they don't really try to reach them. Financial independence, for example, is a goal that is beyond most people's self-confidence.

How do you build your self-confidence? Consider a little character who looks like a circle with a slice cut out for a mouth. He used to be called a munchie but has been popularized as PacMan. If the little munchie goes out and tries to swallow a great big goal, he can't do it—he's not big enough. But that's the situation most people are in. They may try, but they usually can't do what they most want to do. So they try and fail, and try and fail, and try and fail, until they get better at failing than they do at trying. Then they quit.

So what's the solution? Well, there are several principles built into this world and into us to allow us to succeed. One is that goals are sequential.

Goals are sequential

The great big goal can be broken down into a smaller one that can be broken down into a smaller one still, until the goal is a size we can manage. Every millionaire I know was first half a millionaire. And before that, a quarter millionaire. And an eighth. And a sixteenth. And a thirty-second. And almost anyone can be a thirty-second of a millionaire, because that's only around $30,000, and you've probably got at least that much tied up in your house and car and furniture—the equity and assets you already own. Just think: you can walk around saying, "Hey, I'm a thirty-second of a millionaire." (Of course, you can't afford a loaf of bread because of inflation, but that's another story.) Now all you have to do is take the next step and become a sixteenth of a millionaire. With a little thought, work, and organization, you may not find that so hard to do. It doesn't take the brains of a nuclear physicist. *It just takes figuring out what your next small step is and doing it.* Then repeat that process enough times until you get to where you want to be.

GOAL

Goals are concentric

What happens when the munchie eats? When he successfully gets a bite out of one of those goals? Well, what happens when you and I eat? We grow. The bowling average moves up to 165. Then we're ready to take on that next bite, and so on, until we've reached the goal. At each step, the self-image pushes up the self-confidence, until the munchie is big enough to swallow the whole goal, and other goals like it. What we must conclude is that the most *important* goal in your whole plan is the one so small and so easy that there is no reason—*no* reason—not to achieve it.

Goals are achievable

WHAT COMES NEXT?

Do you know what that next small goal is for you? Identifying it is critical because:

1. If your next step is realistic, your whole goal is realistic. That doesn't necessarily mean you will *reach* your ultimate goal, but it does mean you can realistically work on it. For example, suppose you want to be elected to a national office. Your plan calls for you to establish yourself in a state-level elected position so you can move on later to a national position. But before you can get into a state position, you believe you will have to be elected to a county office and become better known. But you have also determined that your neighborhood party committee is the source of elected officials for your county. So, if your *next* step—to be elected to the neighborhood committee—is realistic, your whole goal is realistic, because you *can*

accomplish the only thing you can work on—getting elected to the neighborhood committee.

2. If your next step is unrealistic, you really have no goals program. We all know dreamers who talk about the millions they are going to make but who can't cover this month's rent, the people who want to heal all of the world's ills but can't seem to get along with their next-door neighbors.

As an anonymous poet wrote:

"Your task, to build a better world," God said.
I answered, "How?
This world is such a large, vast place,
    so complicated now.
And I so small and useless am,
There's nothing I can do."
But God in all his wisdom said,
"Just build a better you."

If you can't take the next step toward your goal, or if you don't even know what it is, how can you ever expect to reach that goal? Too many of us are like the members of Procrastinators International; they are fully committed to their cause, but they just can't get a meeting scheduled to organize and do anything about it.

Why not take a few minutes right now to list the next step for your most important goals? You may find yourself motivated to work on something that you have put off for a long time because you thought it was too big or too hard. But the next step isn't hard—you can make it as small and as easy as you want.

JUST ASK

You may not have a dime in your pocket, but you can still go down to the bank and ask, "How much do I have to deposit every month to give my kid a college education?" But most people won't do it. More people fail because they are unwilling to *find out* the price than *ever* fail because they are unwilling to *pay* the price. Many people are living in apartments today because they are afraid to go ask what a house would cost—even though the down payment and monthly payments might be no more than the monthly rent on their apartment. The problem is, they are afraid to find out. They don't think they will be able to afford it, and their self-confidence is so low that they don't dare ask.

Did you go to Hawaii last year? Why not? Probably figured you couldn't afford it—low self-image, low self-confidence. Did you call the travel agent and ask about the different options available? Probably didn't even consider it. But you might have been surprised. Or maybe not. But what could you lose by asking?

I have a client who drives Lincolns. He said to me one day, "You know, I've always wanted a Mercedes."

Remembering my experience with the Corvette, I asked, "How much would it take to get one?"

"I don't know," he said. "I've never asked."

Now, I haven't asked either. But I'd be willing to bet that on any given day, you can drive down to your Mercedes dealer and, because of the increased residual value of the car, lease a Mercedes for within thirty dollars of the monthly lease on a Lincoln. The point is that for years my client had been denying himself one of his dreams simply because he'd been unwilling to find out the price. If he'd gone down and checked and *then* decided he couldn't afford it, it wouldn't bother me so much. But I just hate to see people give up on their dreams before they even find out if they're within the range of possibility. And it disturbs me to think about how often we probably do that.

In what areas do you need to build your self-image? In what areas do you need to build the self-image of your team? While you are thinking about it, why not let your imagination soar? Because the truth is, almost anything is open to you as you build your self-image—if you take it one step at a time.

12

OVERCOMING THE FEAR OF THE OBVIOUS

The phone rang in the middle of a hectic Monday morning. "You don't know me," the caller began hesitantly, and something in his tone more than in his words told me he needed help. "I know one of your more prominent clients," he continued, "and he felt you could help me." The caller told me he was forty-two years old, happily married, with a son graduating from high school; he had two other children, a small mortgage, and a new set of Ping golf clubs. The demographics began to take shape. "Could I spend some time talking with you?" he asked. That inner voice I have come to respect and heed prompted me to say yes.

"Could we talk during an afternoon or in the evening?" I asked, knowing that the next day I had a three-hour drive with four hours of client consultation. But there was time in there somewhere for us to plant some seeds and see if they would take root.

"Anything," was his reply, and so he decided to come along for the ride.

What questions could I ask him? Many came to mind: "What patterns in your life are set and which can be changed?" "Are your inconsistencies consistent in their application?" "Where is your motivation?" "What is your fear?" "What causes you to act or not act?" "What do you do when your heart won't let you do what your mind knows is right?"

"What has been your income pattern over the past five years?" I asked.

"Well, the best year I had was three years ago, and I made $78,000." Hadn't he heard the question?

"And currently?" I asked.

Sheepishly he replied, "Well, I've sold only one policy this year, and that has brought me $18,000 in commissions. But this is only May, and I'm living in a house I can afford."

What is this guy? I thought. *Un-American?*

"So I've got time to sell what I need to. The problem is, I'm afraid I won't do it. I'm burned out on my business," he went on, "but I love to play. I'll play golf at the drop of a tee."

"What are your goals?" I asked.

"When?"

"Next week."

"I don't know. I wake up in the middle of the night and can't sleep."

"Why?"

"Fear, and thinking I'm not going to make the grade."

"How is that possible?"

"I've never been on the straight track. I graduated from high school with a 1.23 overall grade point average. Then I struggled with going into a two-year volunteer commitment for my church. Once I was involved, I loved it tremendously, but I realize now that it was just a delaying tactic to avoid this terrifying process called life.

"When my leader in this experience committed me to attend college, I told him no way. I thought I had precluded that option with my 1.23 grade point average. But he insisted, and with my newly found maturity, I was accepted to a college and graduated a few years later with a 3.2 grade point average. Next came a good job with a brokerage firm, a rookie-of-the-year award, and an income inconceivable to me just a few years before. Sounds like the American dream—wife, kids, home in the suburbs. But I have no ability or desire or application to keep it going. I can't decide if I'm having a bad year or just an off month.

I'm trying to figure out if my income is down because of the month I took off or because one of the months I worked just didn't pan out."

AVOIDING RESPONSIBILITY

Isn't it amazing how we can assess blame to a nonpersonal entity like the month business is "just off"? As he continued to talk, I began to notice a pattern: he was avoiding the obvious things he needed to do with his life.

"I moved out of the office of the major carrier of life insurance that I sell," he went on, "and moved into an office in my home.

"Why?" I asked.

"Well, my last house had a beautiful office, and I wanted to be closer to the kids.

"And now?" I asked.

"Well, just to keep the expenses down and, you know, to . . . uh . . . "

"To keep from having to produce too much?" I interjected.

He nodded. "Yeah, that's probably it."

All of his questions were the kind no one could be held accountable for answering; he kept trying to ask deeply philosophical questions about the meaning of life—questions that don't help much in solving the kinds of problems he needed to deal with.

Such avoidance of responsibility is actually fairly common because once we decide where we want to go, we are responsible for the consequences of our choices. Otherwise, making the decision would be easy. For example, I can put fifteen people into a room and give them a decision-making test, and they'll be real good at it. Jaguar or Corvette? No problem. Blond or brunette? Easy choice. Tennis or golf? Got it. They can check off those choices in nothing flat. Why? Because anyone can make decisions *when there are no real consequences to those decisions*. That's why the CEO who has no trouble deciding to approve a ten-million-dollar budget may not be able to answer a simple question from a new friend who calls on the phone:

Friend: "Where are we going out tonight?"

CEO: "I don't know. Where would *you* like to go?"

Friend: "Well, it really doesn't matter to me. What are you planning on wearing?"

CEO: "Well, what are *you* wearing?"

And on it goes. What makes the difference? The budget decision will have little effect on the executive's personal life, but the dinner date—well, that's a different matter. The difference lies in how much we *care* about the consequences of our choices.

The other thing to keep in mind about choices is that we are built with better decision-making ability, with better *agency*, than we are usually willing to admit. For example, suppose you are driving your six-thousand-pound car thirty miles an hour down a residential street when a six-ounce red rubber ball bounces out from between two parked cars. What do you do? You immediately *stop*, because you know that the next thing to bounce out into the street will be a three-year-old child trying to get the ball back. It's an easy decision.

But my new friend was trying in every way he could to avoid making decisions. So I continued to probe. "Where do you want to be when you are fifty-five years old?" I asked.

"Oh, that's too far away from now. I'm not even sure I want to stay in this industry."

"I didn't ask where you *don't* want to be but where you *do* want to be."

The Need for Small, Positive Goals

Now, this may seem obvious to you, but apparently it is not obvious to many people: you cannot achieve a negative goal. I am amazed at how often people describe success as an absence of something. The human mind cannot imagine the absence of a destination. Even if you describe your future in terms of "at least as much as . . . " rather than "I don't want any less than I'm getting now," you have at least given your mind something to work toward. A terrible message for the mind is "I have no idea," and even worse is "I don't care." These messages cause a complete system shutdown and absolution from all responsibility for action. They cause fear.

Fear is paralyzing. It is overwhelming. It is:

False   Evidence   Appearing   Real

Its worst result is the sense of total inability to act—of seeing the worst in every situation and the futility of any action. It brings the feeling that everything—the problem, the solution, even life itself—is overwhelming. How can you break through? Start somewhere, *anywhere*, and conquer something, *no matter how small*. With this success comes new-found courage to continue.

I had to help my friend stop his slide into despondency. Hopelessness breeds inaction, and the inaction confirms the hopelessness, which further inhibits the behavior necessary to break the downward spiral.

People who feel hopeless ask questions like, "What can I possibly do?" "How big a turnaround do I have to make?" "Do I need a career change?" "Can anyone do it?" "Has anyone ever done it?" These questions are all in the extreme. Why? Because if I can make the problem large enough, then no one can expect me to solve it. Obvious, yes, but all solutions start with the little changes—not the major turnarounds but rather the minor adjustments that seem almost insignificant. The person under the negative influence of fear says, "What good will that do? I suppose I could make that small change, but that won't make this problem (which I have expanded into an end-of-the-world magnitude) go away." This expand-the-problem-to-the-unsolvable state is essential to the paralysis mode.

No matter how high you have risen, when the fear demon grabs your throat you think in extremes, and those extremes tend to be negative. *Solve the problem in the smallest possible increment.*

Obvious? Not necessarily to all. Why do gamblers try to win back all their money at once? Why, when we are feeling the worst about ourselves, do we go for the big score?

Divide and Conquer

If we can learn to see our fear for what it is, we can also begin to solve our problems. How? Divide and conquer. If I want to make $100,000 a year, and I am willing to put in a normal 240 days after vacation and holidays, I want to make $417 per day. Now, maybe your deals don't come in $417 packages. Then convert the numbers to the required frequency of transactions at your current average income and set yourself up to win in the smallest possible increment of success. You see, my friend was not having a problem closing sales. No, his problem was in not *opening* cases, not making the calls on the front end.

I explained all this to him and suggested that he needed to face up to the realities of his life. Then I asked him what small increment of his problem he could work on to do that. He was surprised at his own reaction: "You know, there *is* something I can do!" he said. "I can make one call to a potential client tonight." Then I knew we were making headway. When the smallest element of self-confidence emerges, we are beginning to win the war on fear.

Building Motivation

The other side of this process is to find a need or want that is greater than the fear of acting. When the greatness of the need or want contrasts with the smallness of the task to be accomplished, we begin to find the motivation to achieve our desired level of success. We might bring to light our increased financial needs in the near future: crystallizing the cost of college or other post–high-school expenditures for the kids; building the desire for the next new house; defining the necessary investment to bring financial independence at a particular age. Even the new set of Ping golf clubs or the prospect of the $59.95 overnight special at the local Marriott can be the beginning of breaking the fear syndrome.

We normally act only to achieve a greater benefit or avoid a greater loss. Breaking the fear syndrome requires the use of both sides of the equation, and the benefit or loss must be tested against the idea of reality in the mind of the participant. So I asked my friend, "Can you go out and make the calls that will result in $417 of daily income? And if you do it for a week, will you celebrate with the overnight weekend?"

"Yes, yes, yes!" he said. The answer came as if we had discovered the secret of the ages. And perhaps we had.

What stops us from using this formula? Do we fear the elementary, childish bribery it implies? Well, I want you to know that I have used this method to help millionaires overcome their motivational glitches and even to avoid falling into a slump in the first place. The best of professional athletes, even with their enormous incomes, still wager small dinners on their ability to perform in the upcoming game. The obvious truth is that winners continue to win at the little things that add up to large victories.

AVOIDING EXCUSES

Within seventy-two hours after our interview, I found myself in a luncheon with yet *another* friend, named Harold, forty-four years old. He had made a miscalculation in a mid-career move, and after a second "oops" he had decided to strike out on his own selling advertising services. His income the previous year had been over $50,000, and he was working on moving to $65,000 in the current year. "What's the concern?" I asked.

"I'm spending too much time in clerical tasks. Consequently, my business is not prospering and developing. I should there's that awful word again be using my considerable skills in more sophisticated endeavors. My talent is greater than this market realizes."

One thing I have learned is that if you don't see the market as appreciating your skills, it is not the market's fault, and using the word *should* to describe behavior in others that you can't control or influence is incredibly short-sighted.

"What do you think the solution is?" I asked.

"Well, I could start an ad agency, but that involves many risks. Besides, I already tried it, and it didn't work."

Of course it didn't work. The goal was too big, and his self-confidence was too small. When our goals or desires are beyond our self-confidence, we become more concerned about what we have to lose than what we have to gain.

What makes a person, allegedly on track for $75,000 a year, stall over the decision to hire a $1,500 a month administrative assistant? "Well, the money's tight. The last time I tried that, I got stuck with a real tough situation, and besides, managing other people is just a pain."

One of the psychological games the coach must avoid at all costs is what psychiatrist Eric Berne calls "Why Don't You—Yes But." He describes the game in this way: "[The game] can be played by any number. The agent [for illustrative purposes named White] presents a problem. The others start to present solutions, each beginning with 'Why don't you . . . ?' To each of these White objects with a 'Yes, but . . . ' A good player can stand off the others indefinitely until they all give up, whereupon White wins. In many situations she might have to handle a dozen or more solutions to engineer the crestfallen silence which signifies her victory." (*Games People Play* [New York: Ballantine Books, 1973], pp. 116-17.)

But rather than play this fruitless game, why not turn the experience into one of self-discovery and commitment to action, no matter how small. Using such questions as "What can you do?" "What will you do?" "What stands in the way of accomplishing that step?" and constantly reducing the problem to its smallest element is the secret of success. If the coach senses resistance to any step, he or she must divide it into the next smallest step and get the player to recommit. Remember: no step is too small when we are reversing the slide of fear.

IDENTIFYING THE FEAR

The other meaningful portion of effective coaching is to identify the *real* fear. Harold used the words *concern, apprehension,* and *worry,* all euphemisms for that worst of all four-letter words: *fear.* Harold acknowledged that a portion of the real concern was that, after he had hired the administrative assistant, he couldn't find enough new business to pay the assistant's salary. Why did those feelings exist? Because, deep down, Harold had not studied his past business practices and did not know what he needed to do to build his business. He had no scorecard, no Results to Resources Ratio that would indicate how much increased effort would be needed to produce the results to justify his investment. Fear almost always has its roots in a lack of information. And fear is multiplied by the concern for avoiding failure, or, more important, the *confirmation* of failure in the mind of the participant. The fear of proving the failure is so strong that we often avoid the possibility of finding out that we can win. Harold needed to retrace his steps, see what he had accomplished in the past, and concentrate on his strengths to revive the confidence to proceed.

DOING WHAT WORKS

The simple truth is that the great and the self-confident usually simply repeat a formula that they know will work. They work the specific demographics that have produced orders before. They experiment with small variations on a well-known theme rather than try to compose huge new symphonies. Game plans that create superbowl victories are forged with small variations on successful plays rather than the grandiose new strategies of the fearful rookie. Tennis research reveals that proven professionals usually take two, three at the most, strategies into championship matches. Good amateur players may take as many as five for each opponent. The mediocre player has twenty-five ways to make it work but not the confidence or commitment to practice even one.

Many years ago, one of the world's great chess masters, Eugene A. Znosko-Borovsky, wrote a little book called *How Not to Play Chess*. In it he said: "It is worse than idle to attempt to anticipate every possible reply your opponent may make to each of your proposed moves. You will but waste your time; in fact you will only lose yourself in a maze of calculations which can have no end. Never, therefore, do what so many less experienced players do in analyzing a position, eternally putting the question to themselves: 'If I do this, he will do that—or that—or that,' ad infinitum! *First form your ideal picture on the supposition that your opponent does nothing.* With this picture clear in your mind, then is the time to ask yourself what general plan your opponent may form to counter yours." ([New York: Dover Publications, 1961], pp. 76-77; italics added.)

In other words, don't become paralyzed by fear. Simply take stock of your situation, figure out what you can do, and let the rest go. Then don't forget to *do* what you have decided you *can* do to realize your plan. Exactly how you are going to reach that ultimate goal may seem a little fuzzy, but don't let that frighten you. *Pay attention to what you can do right now.* As the chess master says: "We must have a definite idea of the object which we wish to attain, and then make our moves with this one idea in view. . . . If you have a definite plan, it will not be difficult to find the move best suited to its furtherance at any particular moment. . . . True, you cannot start a game with a complete detailed plan in your mind, *but you can have a general aim, which will give you your orientation, and with every move your aim will become more definite.* . . . Hold to your main idea, however difficult the position may seem. If you are forced to abandon it, you will have to bow to the inevitable, for necessity knows no law. *But you must not too readily sub-*

mit to the conclusion that you are so forced. This would mean that you considered that your opponent had already outplayed you. If, however, a careful analysis of the position convinces that you stand as well as he does, do not tamely submit to his will. A way must be sought . . . to meet the enemy threat and at the same time further your main plan. Of course, if you have no definite plan you are beaten before you begin to play. If you have, do not too readily admit to an inferiority complex." (Ibid., pp. 51-52, 61; italics added.)

In life, as in chess, the destruction of fear begins with a decision about what you really want, followed by taking the necessary steps, one by one, to obtain it. The goal may not be easy, but it need not be overwhelming. You can overcome your fear of the obvious and achieve your goals, one step at a time.

13

THE OBVIOUS POWER OF GOALS

One day as a traveler drove down a country road in Kansas, he happened upon a barn with twelve targets painted on it, and precisely in the center of each target was an arrow. "What skill this modern-day Robin Hood must possess!" thought the traveler. "I would dearly love to meet such a talent." No sooner had the thought disappeared than its object came into view. Across the meadow walked a young man with a bow and an appropriately empty quiver.

"Son, are you the archer whose handiwork I observed upon the barn?"

" 'Tis I," replied the lad.

"What skill, what dedication!" the impressed traveler offered admiringly. "It must require much practice."

"Not so much," replied the lad, "since I started painting the targets after I shot the arrows!"

THREE LEVELS IN SETTING GOALS

Well, that's one person who knew how to bring his performance in line with his goals. But that's not exactly the way we want to do it. We can commit our business team to greater levels of performance over longer periods of time by using the following new approach to goal setting. We can set goals in three ranges:

1. Certainty.
2. Probability.
3. Possibility.

By using these common risk-assessment terms, we lower the level of abstraction in our thinking and increase our team's level of understanding and commitment.

CERTAINTY

Certainty is the level everyone can agree on, the level of reliability. It brings memories of Robert Blake's portrayal of television character Tony Baretta and his trademark phrase: "And you can take that to the bank!" This phrase has various regional parallels, such as the southeastern United States comment "It's a done deal." This level is so simple, so easy, and, most important, so believable to the performers that no one questions it. "A level that everyone agrees on is too low," some say, and they may have a point. But more often than not, when a team commits to a performance level they are certain they can reach, they work harder to meet that commitment. Then, as they succeed, they grow in their self-confidence and self-esteem and their desire to move on to higher levels. What a blessed alternative to the old "bet 'em high, then sleep in the streets" philosophy my father describes from his wild, single sailor days!

It is all right to take people where they are, get them to agree on their target, and help them to hit it—although not to the extent of the young archer in Kansas. That is not the level of certainty we are looking for. But it is the kind we find in too many circumstances where the bet-'em-high philosophy exists. We may occasionally berate the team for failing to reach a goal. But in the long term, if we accept the obvious principle that *the behavior we wish to have repeated must be reinforced*, then the enlightened approach of set it/hit it, set it/hit it, is the best one for the team. Please remember, success is, in some significant portion, made up of planned, practiced patience, and with this certainty level, people's natural desire to be better than they used to be will keep them on the trail to improvement.

Another benefit to establishing this minimum certainty level is that success is often as much the achievement of a level of performance as it is the achievement of a point. For example, the commitment that "the financial statement will be out no later than the tenth working day after the close of the accounting period" establishes the minimum level of performance, and it is something management can count on, something they can take to the bank. An accounting team that consistently sets and hits the tenth day will naturally be drawn to improve that level after two or three successful completions. And the wonderful thing is that they own the goal when they are the ones who want to improve.

PROBABILITY

On the level of probability, again we find power in the simplicity and common understanding of the word in everyday usage. Again taking the example of the financial statement, the team will be willing to commit that "probably" the statement will be out on the tenth working day following the close of the period. In other words, as far as we know there is no good reason for this *not* to happen. This common understanding may not be a complete agreement on what is needed. Still, it is the basis for a slight increase in commitment in exchange for the understanding that "my life is not on the line for this level of performance, but I recognize that the level of celebration is increased." If the level is not met, we will be disappointed but not devastated. As a friend of mine says, "If we don't make it, no one will die." This *elimination of the fear of punishment* creates increased emotional incentive for the team to stretch. Another critical element of this system is that the praise be appropriate to the performance *as compared to the expectation*. Also, people are often willing to accept the challenge of this level of accomplishment if you can show them that they have done it in the past. When they know they have done it, they are more likely to believe they can do it again. It is a probable level of performance.

Possibility

The highest level of goal commitment is the possibility level, often referred to as the dream level. I believe that the enlightened term of *possible* takes advantage of the common usage and understanding of that word. The common terminology "in your dreams" is indicative of the improbability we associate with the term. Conversely, the term *possible* at least introduces the performance level into the realm of "perhaps."

This level may be compared to the junior-high-school opportunity in English class to turn in book reports for extra credit. Somehow we believe that the absence of the project does not reflect negatively on our grade but that the extra credit is awfully nice. The natural extension of this course of action is that the scorecard reflects the continued improvement and the desire to be better than we used to be, naturally increasing commitment. The two obvious forces at work in this example are the *believability of the goals* and the *individual choice of the levels*.

The most important issue at this level is patience. Letting the players see that their performance could improve (and without negative consequences if they fail) begins to stretch their horizons. When a record game is in progress during a certain time frame (such as a week, a month, or a year), the existence of the possibility level gives us a place to shoot for once the probability level is reached. A great friend and coach, Rex Houze, says, "If you can do it once, you can do it twice, and if you can do it twice, you can turn it into a habit." The existence of the possibility level in our goals program makes that philosophy work and builds the performance of the team beyond any level they are currently willing to commit to.

Periodically, the possibility level is achieved by accident or by unanticipated performance. In the 1970s, we had the opportunity to work with a soft-drink bottler. Among the many scorecards we created was one for the bottle sorters. This was not a glamorous position, not a career position, not even a place we could keep staffed with great regularity. But this became an opportunity to turn adversity into advantage. The five-person team was achieving just over thirty-two cases of bottles sorted per worker hour. This seemed to be an acceptable pace, especially since management had no idea of what the past performance had been. Then we had a fortuitous day—one of the workers was absent! Because of the pressure of the queue, the line needed more bottles to fill. The reduced four-man crew produced almost as many cases for the shift as the average produced by the five-man group. The previous daily average was 1,280 cases per day divided by 5 workers divided by 8 hours = 32 cases sorted per worker per hour.

On the day of the absenteeism, production was 1,216 cases divided by the 4 workers divided by 8 hours = 38 cases sorted per worker per hour. Incredible! Reproducible on a consistent basis? Probably not. But possible! A new measurement stake had been placed in the ground. Of course, the overall cumulative average increased (creating an impact on what the probability level would be in the future). But most important, a new high-water mark was on the scorecard—undeniable proof that a higher level of achievement was possible by *this* team on *this* assignment in *this* company with its unique corporate culture.

When the absent worker returned to the job, what happened? Naturally, the team pointed out how well they had done without him, and the peer pressure for attendance was a lovely side benefit. More important, the entire team responded to the opportunity to create a new record— which they did just a few short weeks later. In addition, when the inevitable employee turnover occurred, the team captain negotiated with management to keep the four-member team and share a portion of the increased savings with the team members. The group continued to improve and exceeded the fifty cases per man hour level within six months of the thirty-eight-case possibility point being established.

It was Henry Ford who said, "Whether you think you can or you think you can't, you're right." The obvious principle of the possibility point introduces a new stretch point to the human psyche, and once the mind accepts the possibility, our inbred desire for progression turns possibility into reality. But, more significantly, until the mind accepts the possibility point, that normal and natural progression and achievement drive cannot and will not turn on.

It is imperative that the coach, upon the creation or accomplishment of a new possibility point, does not imply or express any expectation that the new point will be repeated with regularity. We have found that one of the hesitancies on the part of the players to celebrate appropriately is the fear that the new momentary achievement level will become the norm. If the coach will develop the patience to allow the team the choice, they will move to much higher levels than could be achieved by expecting immediate perfection.

This topic of possibility points and thinking fuels another powerful and obvious principle of people-powered motivation, that of recording, recognizing, and enthusiastically celebrating personal bests.

THE ULTIMATE POSSIBILITY POINT

The plaque hanging in the neighborhood Golden Arches commemorating the "record lunch" or best dinner hour or largest order served creates a special pride for the entire team to look up to and remember. Sure we acknowledge that it was an exception. But with same breath, even the same words, we acknowledge that it was an exceptional feat accomplished by exceptional people. It is remembered with that special pride reserved for Super Bowls and world championship performances, with a special desire to be repeated. This is what constitutes bragging rights, the stuff we show to Mom when she comes to see the place we work.

In 1985, Larry Martin, executive vice-president of Martin Door Manufacturing, Inc., in Salt Lake City, Utah, had a thriving business manufacturing large garage and industrial doors from 3,000-foot rolls of steel. But one question Larry wondered about was how much steel was being wasted in the production process. To find out, he asked the workers to start tracking the waste material, which they did. At the time, similar plants expected to waste around 4 percent, or 120 feet out of every 3,000-foot roll. Larry's group came in at a highly efficient 2 percent. He was pleased, of course, but he challenged them to do even better—would three-fourths of a percent be possible? They didn't know, but they started to work on it. As they did, they found that they needed to pay attention to many different details: how to unload the steel from the truck to minimize damage, how to handle the steel once it was in the plant, and many other factors. They became more and more efficient, but they kept wondering if they could do even better. They started to think not only about percentages but also about how much of each *individual roll* they could keep from wasting. They modified their existing machines to work more efficiently, and they asked Larry to bring in additional machines to make further improvement possible. A year later, on November 17, 1986, they brought Larry their crowning achievement—the world's record for smallest amount of waste from a roll of steel. Thirty feet (1 percent of a roll) would have been superb. Twenty-five feet would have been fantastic. Twenty feet would have been impossible. They presented Larry with a piece of steel twenty-seven *inches* long. Larry mounted the tiny thing on a wooden plaque and hung it on the wall, and it has been a main attraction during every plant tour for the sixth grade, the families of the employees, and, I might add, all visiting dignitaries. Some of the team members have departed and some have been promoted, but their names are recorded for posterity on the plaque, and their record still stands—the stuff of which stories for grandchildren are made. Perhaps equally amazing is the fact that the team also set a record for work efficiency for that time. Seven hundred pounds of steel per worker hour was considered pretty good, but they were up to 1,040 pounds per worker hour. A happy accident? No. These spectacular results came from setting and working toward clear, specific goals.

14

Empowering Growth in Your Team

Charles Percy, business leader and former senator from Illinois, was elected president and CEO of Bell and Howell at the tender age of twenty-nine. On this auspicious occasion, he was interviewed by a national business newspaper, and the conversation went something like this:

Reporter: "How did you make this incredible jump in such a short time?"

Percy: "I read the book."

Reporter: "What do you mean?"

Percy: "When I got my first position at Bell and Howell, I applied the standard time-management principles:

1. Itemize. I listed the results I wanted and the tasks required to achieve them.

2. Categorize. I put similar items together.

3. Prioritize. I decided what things were most important and which ones could be put aside for later.

4. Delegate or eliminate. I decided on what could better be done by someone else and, more important, what didn't have to be done at all."

Reporter: "What's so unusual about that?"

Percy: "Some might find it unusual that I delegated or eliminated *everything*."

Reporter: "*Everything?* Weren't you worried about having nothing to do?"

Percy: "No, not for long."

Reporter: "What happened?"

Percy: "Interestingly enough, another position opened up in the department. When the personnel manager called down for the specifications to begin the hiring search, my manager said, 'We don't need to hire anyone. Let's just give the job to Percy. He doesn't have anything to do.' "

Reporter: "What did you do then?"

Percy: "The same thing I did before: I itemized, categorized, prioritized, and delegated or eliminated."

Reporter: "How much of your work did you delegate or eliminate this time?"

Percy: "All of it."

Reporter: "Didn't that worry you?"

Percy: "Not really. Before long, the department manager's position became available. When the personnel manager called down for the position specifications, the boss said, 'We don't need to hire anybody. We'll just give the job to Percy. He doesn't have anything to do.' This went on for some time, until, five years later, the board of directors was looking for a new chief executive officer. Guess what they said: "Let's give the job to Percy. He doesn't have anything to do.' "

THE BASIS FOR MEASURING PROGRESS

What do you think about Charles Percy's story? Was he just being lazy? Was he taking advantage of others? Or was he actually helping others grow? Maybe delegating all of that additional responsibility to others was the best thing he could have done, helping them to progress while giving him a chance to focus on bigger issues.

What is best in any given situation is not always clear, and people sometimes have a misperception about what constitutes the proper basis for measuring progress. Historically we have been told that we should always strive to do our best—which I believe Percy, despite his self-deprecating story, did. The Bible even tells us, "Be ye therefore perfect," a tall order and frankly not one containing much sense of progress. If perfection is the standard, then I am doomed to a no-way-to-win conclusion.

Think about how we use the word *best*. Its definition suggests that it would properly be followed by a period, as the absolute term it rightly is. However, consider these typical uses of the word: "I was the best of the class of 1962." "Be the best you can." "The best of the show." "The best of the team." "The best we have." Each example includes a modifying phrase that softens the bluntness of the word *best*. Why? Because, as mortals, we cannot hold ourselves accountable to the lofty ideal of perfection.

When we set our goals to be the best, we are setting ourselves up to fail, because of the elusive nature of the very concept we seek. True, the concept is a noble one, but it is discouraging as the basis for measuring success. Perhaps the more disappointing portion is the fact that "be the best" denies the very basis of progression that is so critical to the human need for purpose. Even if the best is accomplished, the victory is momentary, and the need for the next challenge appears.

BEING BETTER THAN EVERYONE ELSE

Closely linked to the above, and bearing all of its liabilities as well as some uniquely its own, is the concept of being better than everyone else. Although lacking the divine distance of "the best," it is nonetheless steeped in illogic and momentary success. Its worst characteristic is the idea that our accomplishments are limited by the quality of our competitors.

Each spring, sixty-four teams line up in the NCAA national basketball tournament. There is invariably a Cinderella team from a small conference who got to the tournament with about twenty-five victories over similar schools. The team lasts one or two rounds, and then their dream of being better than all of the others is dashed. Why? Because their past successes are built on competition at a level below that required to win in that more competitive environment. Or perhaps the point is better made if we consider a perennial conference champion who cannot be competitive in post-season bowl games. Why? Because the accomplishment is limited by the competition.

This can be just as clearly observed in business or social circles. I, for one, would not like my ceiling of self-development set by the people I am competing against.

For years I admired the courage of independent college basketball teams that would play a home-and-home series with UCLA in the John Wooden dynasty years. When asked why they would subject their teams to that level of competition (and most often defeat), one coach replied, "We have no conference to win. The NCAA is all there is for us, and these are the people we need to beat to win the championship." At least if you are forced to use that criteria, you can select the best competition.

THE FASTEST GUN IN THE WEST

The second drawback is the idea of having to be the "fastest gun in the West." It's a problem because, in the modern world, there is always someone faster than you are. There is always new technology, an unexpected shift in the habits of a major customer, or a new regulation, law, or ruling. These all produce the elusive victory, but it is hollow since we know we may not have control over our ability to repeat the success.

"YOU DON'T UNDERSTAND MY TERRITORY"

This third method of comparison, especially if used on a team of key people, results in complaints of "you don't understand my territory." A form of the resistance philosophy of NIH (not invented here), this generates more excuse-making and downright rejection of the concept out of hand than any other reaction. When a regional sales manager returns from the annual meeting with figures showing the national average production per sales representative and attempts to use them to motivate his or her group, the cries and moans resound throughout the hall. "That might work where the economy is stronger," they say, "but here we have to deal with the weather, the government, the competition, and the fact that the national ad campaign doesn't reach our prospects." Translated, that means, "You don't understand my territory." Truly the most important ingredient in any scorekeeping or measurement system is credibility. It is more important even than accuracy. It breeds the believability that provides the motivation to perform, to want to participate.

It breaks down into "I may not be better than the ones you are comparing me to, but I'm not as bad a lot of others." This is the other side of the two-edged sword. While the manager or coach is attempting to get the fourth-place team to tackle the challenge of being number one, the players want to talk about how far they are out of ninth place. As with two ships passing in the night, no communication takes place.

All players want a way to win. That is obvious, and the players will reject any system that denies that right. The other principle at work here is the obvious benefit of maximizing the number of winners in any system. If I have fifteen, or even five, people in a group, and I want to reinforce the behavior I want repeated, the more winners I can produce in each round or period of scorekeeping, the more enthusiastic participants I have for the next round.

"Am I Better Than I Used to Be?"

To capture the benefits of the application of these concepts, I suggest the following question as the only basis for judging accomplishment and growth in human potential or success: Am I better than I used to be? This is the basis for progression and its accompanying sense of purpose. It eliminates the liabilities of the two preceding systems and has the double benefit of eliminating participant rejection and, at the same time, reducing all excuses for non-performance. When my progress is compared primarily, and this a key concept, to my own past performance, I have nowhere to hide; not behind the fairness of the system or any of the outside parameters that allow the convenient rationalizations listed above. The results and the basis for judging success are mine: my territory, my customers, my competitors, and my economy.

The obvious power of this method is apparent in the massive popularity of the game of golf, where only 5 percent of the participants can score less than 90 on a par-72 golf course. Think about it: the majority of participants cannot perform within 120 percent of the ideal established by the course designers, but, because they are out to better their own best or average performance, golf is the fastest growing of the leisure pursuits. Would it have anywhere near the popularity it does if every time you came off the course, the only score delivered by the only scorekeeper was how far short of acceptance or excellence you had performed? Somehow I don't believe that "You're 20 percent below standard" would bring back the bogie shooters in the droves we have come to see in the game. No, it is the believability of winning, the chance for success, that gives people the desire to participate.

Think of the tremendous upsurge in running as a pastime. In the New York City Marathon, more than 20,000 participants run, and another 30,000 are turned down each season. That is 50,000 people with the lifelong dream of running through the Big Apple, without even a mugger chasing them. But why? After all, only one winner is possible, or maybe eight if you include all of the different classes. So what are these nuts doing? Certainly some of them are in it for the association. Some of them want the T-shirts and the bragging rights of finishing. But with the world record at two hours and four minutes, less than a handful can be considered legitimate candidates for the winner's crown. The majority are running for a personal best, a performance that is better than they have done in the past. If you doubt this obvious principle, reflect with me just a minute on what would happen if the organizers shut off the clock after the first six people finished. Not very many would return. Most would quit as the news spread down the course, and all would be up in arms over the change in rules without their prior approval.

Health clubs work on this simple principle, adding more weight or repetitions than the person mastered last time. Reflect on the principle; it becomes obvious with thought. Then begin to change the way you manage or coach to emphasize the betterment of each member of your team, and the results will be amazing. When you have several players with the same scorecards, such as a district sales team or group of retail stores reporting to the same coach, the switch in emphasis is spectacular. Note the following example of improvement in the average size of sale in a retail store group:

ASYMPTOTE STORE SALES PER CUSTOMER
PERIOD 2 COMPARED TO PERIOD 1

FORCED RANKINGS

In a monthly meeting of the managers in a twenty-five-store bookstore chain, the retail vice-president hands out a listing of the stores, ranked by profitability for the past month. The stores are expected to maintain a gross profit margin of 40 percent, and when the list is passed out, the response is something to behold. The three managers whose stores are in prime retail locations have reached a 45-percent profit margin, and they ease back into their chairs with a smile and a sense of smug satisfaction that once again they are at the top of the list. This is the group I call the "loafers." They always feel pretty good about their "accomplishment," but the fact is that any of the managers could do as well as they do—if they had their locations. Their superior performance is based almost completely on the luck of the draw. Oblivious to that fact, however, the vice-president heaps them with laurels and honor.

The second group is made up of the managers who reached 40 percent or just barely above it. "Whew," they think, "glad I made that one." Because they just barely managed to evade the bullet of failure, I call them the "dodgers." They, too, receive the acclamation of their chief.

The third group comprises the ten managers who almost made it, but not quite. Their performance may have been at 39.5 percent, a half percent lower than the lowest performer in the second group, but they are subjected to scorn and derision. I call this group the "strivers" because they are continually working to make the grade. "Someday, somehow," they vow, "I will make it." In actuality, again because of the luck of the draw, there may be no way for them to make it. But the goal is always out there, just beyond their grasp.

The forth group I call the "waiters." Their profit margin is so low that they have given up all hope of ever doing any better and are simply waiting for something to change. Who knows? Maybe one of the better managerial slots will open up and they'll get a new location. In the meantime, they are the pariahs of the entire company.

What's wrong here? All of the groups are victims of a forced ranking. And a forced ranking never works, because it's like comparing apples to oranges. The loafers, because of their comfy situation, will never achieve the kind of performance they might. What if they were working as hard as the strivers? Could they achieve a 50- or even a 60-percent profit margin? The dodgers are so busy trying to avoid failure that they fail to see how they might succeed beyond their wildest dreams. As long as they are over the line, they are all right. But mediocrity is always sad. The strivers, actually the hardest workers of the bunch, will never receive the rewards they so richly deserve for their devoted service in the face of adversity. And the waiters—well, they have simply given up.

It's like the college class that is graded on the curve. If three geniuses sign up, everybody else is in trouble no matter how hard they try.

What's the solution? Get rid of the forced rankings. Instead of comparing the groups with each other, compare each group with its own past performance. That makes it possible to see who is really winning and losing and to do something about it.

TWO INSURANCE AGENTS

In a local office of a national life-insurance company, two agents sit in adjoining offices. They sell the same product lines with the same national advertising, the same sales manager, the same market, the same sales climate. But one of the agents earns ten times the income of the other. What makes the difference? The lower earner is a hard worker. In fact, he spends enough time away from home that it creates resentment in his spouse and children. He makes sales calls regularly, his closing average is better than the office average, and his persistence and administration numbers are among the top 10 percent of veteran agents. He puts in the time and energy necessary to write three policies a week, which he sells to people he is comfortable being around. Like all good agents, he asks for referrals, who turn out to be just like the other people he sells to and, incidentally, just like himself. The trouble is, he doesn't believe he can sell a whole-life policy with a face value of over $10,000.

The top performer is in the office about three days a week on the two weeks out of the month he chooses to show up. He works most intently between the two ski seasons—water and snow—which gives him almost two full months on each end to produce. What, then, makes the difference in production and compensation between the two agents? The size of the deal.

On the advice of a great mentor early in his career, the top producer learned to sell to the people who can afford and who understand the need for his financial products and services. He selected his market, built his prospect file, and selected his country club and other leisure activities to help increase the size of the deal. And to help ensure the accomplishment of his goal, he decided to work around millionaires and potential millionaires—people who had something to protect and something to manage. He consciously built the size of the deal. And when he found he could be successful in that environment, he kept selling in that environment, succeeding again and again.

What is the obvious challenge for the sales manager in that insurance office? Helping the mediocre producer to see the light and grab a larger share of the bounty that is there for the taking. The history of the mediocre performer is filled with successes and failures, moments of joy and moments of disappointment. But he needs to look at that history in a different way and pull the obviously positive performances out of it as inspiration for future success.

As the insurance agent began to examine his sales in descending order of their economic importance, a definite pattern of his real "top end" performance began to emerge. He found several similarities in income level, family size, occupation, leisure activities, clubs, and even church affiliation among his best customers. That was the intellectual conclusion. The greater understanding, the emotional breakthrough, was that he *could* sell large policies. Even though his average commission was only $350 per policy written, still 80 percent of that income, or $28,000, came from twenty-two exceptional cases where the commission was above $1,300 per policy. And the most important part was that these were policies *he* had sold—he himself, in his market, with his prospects, with his products, with his skill. The breakthrough was amazing! He learned that he could find larger cases than the average. Some people *did* want to talk to him, and the numbers were proof positive that he could do it. He had already done it, so he knew he could do it again. He couldn't do it all of the time yet, but he had done it a few times, and he could repeat his performance.

Armed with this new knowledge and improved self-image, the salesman called on the people in the 20-percent category and asked to be referred to their friends. And while he was at it, he asked these people for a larger share of their insurance needs. Why the change? Because possibility thinking was turning into probability thinking, and that thinking prompted action.

BUILDING THE TEAM'S SELF-IMAGE

How do you build the self-image of members of your team? How do you help them boost their performance to new heights? The two main ways are:

1. Constantly remind them of what they do right.

2. Create the possibility of greatness by reinforcing those occasional demonstrations of exceptional performance.

A powerful tool to help you do these two things is found in the asymptote, which is the shape of the curve created by the 80/20 analysis known widely as the Pareto Principle, named for Italian sociologist and economist Vilfredo Pareto. The basic idea of this principle is that in any situation, 20 percent of the resources produces 80 percent of the results. The other 80 percent of the resources produces the remaining 20 percent of the results. You can find examples of this principle almost everywhere you look. For example, 80 percent of your sales probably come from 20 percent of your customers. For years, we have used this principle to determine where our business is coming from and to study the possibility of better using our current client base. But in our recent work, we have discovered another and perhaps even greater application of this principle—stretching the self-image of people on our business team.

I have long stated that in sales and entrepreneurship, the size of the deal is determined primarily by the size of the dealer. What I mean by "size of the dealer" is the level of the dealer's self-image. Some people are just more comfortable selling products with a low price that they can readily see the value of. This allows them to have the intensity to sell the product or service. Luxury car salespeople, for example, see themselves in a different light from those who sell compact cars. And it is a wise coach who matches players to the size of the deal while constantly working to develop and empower all the players.

EMPOWERING YOUR TEAM

Obviously, to gain empowerment a team needs:
1. Clear understanding of the results that are required.
2. Feedback on their performance.
3. The excessive faith and trust of their coach.
4. The opportunity to risk and fail without being considered failures.

Charles Percy, whom we discussed at the beginning of this chapter, was the master of letting people fail and therefore letting them succeed.

It has been said the key to effective management is to first decide what you are going to *stop* doing. Take a moment to look through your personal planner. What areas and tasks can you let go of? What will not suffer if it is done by others? What might actually be done *better* by someone else? Then make a list of five duties, projects, or assignments that could be taken on by each of your team members. Imagine how much easier your life will be when even half of the team respond to even half of the items on your list. Imagine what could happen if you were willing to repeat this process every ninety days! What may be obvious only to those committed to empowerment is that the delegation of responsibility, like all of life, is a process, not to be accomplished in a single seminar or retreat but to be carved out and created in a continuous series of steps. And please remember that those steps must be small enough to be handled by the individual player. I am always asked, "What if the team cannot or will not handle the plan ahead of them? How long do you work with them, Chuck?"

The answer is in the question! You work with them for as long as you are willing to do so. If you have the next step clearly outlined for each team member, and each member is making progress toward the accomplishment of that step, in my judgment the team is entitled to keep on trying. If, on the other hand, you have people on your team for whom you are unwilling to outline the next step, or people who are unwilling to take the next step, then you are doing them and yourself and your organization an extreme disservice by keeping them on board. Trust your instincts as the coach; your instincts helped you get where you are. But please do not keep players on the team who are not getting your feedback and attention and a plan for making them even more valuable than they are now. Remember that people development, like land development, is based on changing the perception of value in the marketplace. Start now to develop and empower the members of your team.

LOOK FOR THE THINGS YOU CAN LET GO OF

The first obvious step in empowering your team may be to get rid of the things you just don't want to do. That is the "courageless" way, but if it gets you started in unburdening you and empowering them, we'll start with that next small step.

After listing the things you would like to get rid of, make a corresponding list of the reasons why those things matter in the first place. Write down at least five reasons why a certain unenjoyable task (or, better still, responsibility) is important to you, to the organization, and, most important, to the player who is going to be responsible for its accomplishment. In doing this, you may find that some of those tasks really don't matter much and can be gotten rid of completely. For the rest, prioritize the reasons behind them in descending order of importance; then explain those reasons when you present the tasks and responsibilities to your players.

Next look at the activities that take most of your time. Resist the temptation to assume that these activities are the ones that are most important. Periodic studies from almost every time-management discipline reveal little relationship between the duration and the importance of a task. In fact, often the contrary seems to be true—the tasks that take the most time are the ones that are most comfortable rather than most important. Again use the list of "whys" to motivate team members to execute the tasks at least as well as you have been doing.

Now begin to really step out. Look for those tasks where your personal involvement actually *slows down* the process. Remember that *wait* is a four-letter word that is best eliminated. Can you convey the reason behind that "just take a look at it, or just approve it" step that causes the team to wait for your schedule before they can make the next move? Can you convey judgment, let them learn, and have them report on the progress at a convenient time? The tricky part of this step is working out the "whys" and perhaps recognizing, somewhat embarrassingly, that there are few if any reasons for keeping those responsibilities to yourself. Remember, "We've always done it that way" is the first reason to change it!

Once you begin to enjoy your increased spare time, take the next risk. Expand the list of "delegatables" to the more important aspects of your responsibility. Look for those areas where you can share the credit, and, as any good coach would, still accept blame as appropriate. You will find that the "whys" in this step are greater and more self-evident and thus more readily accepted by the team.

Next take the plunge of real empowerment. *Ask* your team, "Which of my responsibilities do you want to be able to handle ninety days from now?" Extend the choice, open the door, expand the options, and you will be rewarded with increased caring, buy-in, and ownership from the members of your team. You will see the wisdom in giving to get. If you can delegate just 5 percent of your tasks each quarter, you will get a completely new function every five years. Challenge, change, and championship performance is waiting. Begin today to make the jump.

15

THE FUTURE IS OBVIOUS

A recently retired father, a bit short on funds and looking at Social Security as his main source of income, pulled his spendthrift son aside at the retirement party. "Son," he said, "there's something I've been wanting to tell you. I hope you'll listen, because I know what I'm talking about."

"What is it, Dad?" the son asked.

The father smoothed back his graying hair, looked his son in the eye, and earnestly replied, "There is a tomorrow."

One obvious thing about the future is that it is coming, and we must start getting ready for it now. Yesterday's behavior gave us yesterday's results; today's behavior gives us today's results. But neither of those will give us what we really want for tomorrow's results. So we have to get ready for the future by doing future behaviors, and the easiest way to get ready for the future is to do future behaviors in the present. As a friend of mine says, "We create tomorrow by what we do today."

One of the first things we need for the future is future information. Buy another book, one I didn't write but wish I had: *The Popcorn Report*, by Faith Popcorn. She and her team have come up with some insights about the future that are marvelous. Reread John Naisbitt's *Re-Inventing the Corporation: Transforming Your Job and Your Company for the New Information Society* and get the tips that will allow you to arrive at your own obvious conclusions and, yes, even predictions about what the future will bring. If you want to arrive first, it is best to be on the leading edge.

ACCELERATING OBSOLESCENCE

Most people are content with today's or yesterday's behaviors. And they pray for tomorrow's results. But if you are not preparing for the future, consider this observation from George Odiorne, creator of management by objectives: "Things that don't change remain the same." He also said, "Things that remain the same quickly become obsolete." Is that what you want to be? If not, why not take a minute, right now, to list five things that have become obsolete in your business in the past ten years. That part is easy. The real challenge, however, is to identify five things that you expect to become obsolete in your business in the next five years, and then to create a plan to change your behavior to prepare for and maybe even accelerate the obsolescence of those items. Remember, *accelerated obsolescence becomes innovation.*

Let's look at an example: cellular communications. I have a cellular phone, but I guarantee it will soon be obsolete—all cellular phones will. Mobile phones have gone through a rapid evolution. When mobile phones first appeared in the early 1970's they cost several thousand dollars and took up nearly half your trunk. Soon they were more compact and the price had dropped by half. Then hand-held telephones came down the pike, followed quickly by cellular service. Prices continued to drop and palm size became the norm. Now, for the promise of a year's service, the phones are free. And the Dick Tracy wrist radio? That, too, is already available. Look at what the leaders are doing in the market: smaller, lighter, more built-in features, greater ease of use—faster, simpler, cheaper.

Take another moment, right now, and list similar adjectives that describe the future trends that will become apparent in the delivery of your product or service, maybe that are already becoming apparent. Try this exercise with a few of your closest associates: brainstorm, list, prioritize, and begin to implement some of these adjectives in your products and services in an effort to accelerate obsolescence. "Why in the world should I try to accelerate obsolescence?" you ask. "I'm trying real hard to do just the opposite—to keep my products and services from becoming obsolete." The point is that if you can anticipate and even create the obsolescence (which is inevitable anyway), you can profit from the obsolescence ahead of the rest of the world.

Another good example is computers. Notebooks and laptops are popular now. A few years ago I paid $3,300 for a luggable sewing-machine sized compact computer. Then I bought an IBM-compatible 286 for $4,300. The year after I bought it, it was worth $2,000. I didn't sell it for $2,000 though. I quibbled over $200. Then it was worth $1,200. Then $800. In the meantime, I bought a 386, but the interesting thing is that it cost less than the 286 I bought a year and a half ago. The half-life of the latest chip number decreases with every generation, and now we can only imagine the number of the chip being conceived in the minds of those marvelous scientists and engineers. My point is that if we anticipate the obsolescence, then we can buy around it or take advantage of it in some other way. In fact, there is undoubtedly a whole new industry of PC traders who are buying and then selling off those old 286 XTs—rolling them out to Russia, rolling them out to the Third World, taking advantage of that obsolescence. Other people try to ignore obsolescence, thinking they won't have to deal with it.

A certain family pizza emporium came into our area in the early 1980s, and it was a fun place to eat—animated figures to entertain while you dined, and a high-tech playground and video games you could enjoy after your meal. Kids loved it, and before long it was so packed you couldn't even get into the place. We met with the people who owned it, and they had a couple of problems. One was bad service—even on a good day. The other was cardboard pizza with rubber sausage and plastic cheese.

The discipline of finding the obvious teaches us to look for clues, warning signs, of impending disaster. So, as obsolescence accelerators, we began to look at what these people were not doing—basic things, such as providing good pizza. It quickly became apparent that they were willing to sit on yesterday's successes rather than prepare for tomorrow's challenges. Armed with our assessment, we met with the owners and said, "Why don't you consider upgrading your goods and services package?"

"Are you crazy?" they asked. "Just look out there! The kids are lined up."

What I told them, and what I'm telling you, is that you can't just be satisfied with the fact that you have a line of people outside your front door. You have to look at how long that line is and at how long the line is in front of your competitor's door. You can't just measure your success at the cash register, because although things look the same inside, outside the line may be getting shorter. You have to keep score every day on the obvious factor of how many people are in line.

A lot of companies live and breathe just by working on marketing strategies, product development, competitive advantage. All that really means is that they are keeping an eye on the future. Somewhere, somebody right now is in a meeting discussing what will be happening with razor blades a year from now, what will be happening with video cassette players five years from now. They're changing their behavior today to meet the edge, while somebody with the cardboard pizza syndrome is saying, "We don't have to worry about tomorrow because we already have the world by the tail." And that's when they get into trouble.

We do have to worry about tomorrow. We have to be making room for the things we want to have come into our lives, room for the future. Remember John Goddard and Lou Holtz and their wish lists? If you haven't made yours yet, it's time to start.

BACK TO THE FUTURE

I believe that in the future, things will be better than they are today—and worse. In fact, we may see an increasing polarization of values in every area of life. However, in many of today's trends I see very promising things about what the future may hold.

One of the most important, and predictable, is the recognition of the value of the customer—although it will come too late for my friends at the defunct pizza parlor. But we are already seeing that people are becoming more important than institutions. This recognition will not be a great new breakthrough but rather a return to the foundation of the free-market economy, not just in the United States but all over the world. My father and his father before him repeated the charge from my earliest years:

Rule 1: The customer is always right.

Rule 2: If you ever think the customer is wrong, see rule number 1.

We will see more customer surveys, more store-specific and neighborhood-specific marketing. We will see more customer input before major changes are made in automobile models or accessories. Good examples are the Taurus project at Ford Motor Company and the Chrysler project of interviewing more than 250,000 owners of their popular mini-vans, even though they were already the leading sellers in that automobile category.

Let's do something about it right now. List your most important customers, external and traditional, or internal and nonconventional. Who relies upon you to get their needs met? Maybe you are the finish grinder in a manufacturing plant or auto body shop. That painter who is responsible for the next step is your customer. Maybe you are in information systems. That manager or other associate waiting for the information is your customer. Look at your customer list and determine what else they want from you. Start by interviewing them, questioning them, getting their direct feedback. Next, step back and look at what happens with your product after they receive it. Could you anticipate the next step and increase the value of your goods or services? A leading cheese product that most of us remember from the 1950s finally in 1992 introduced its product in single-serving microwavable packaging. Yet its customers have been heating, pouring, and dipping that product for decades. Photocopy machines that collate, staple, and even bind reflect that same sensitivity to anticipated customer services. And you must continue to be ahead of that customer. Studebaker was the leading maker of horse-drawn wagons in the late 1800s. They made the transition to automobiles but then missed the assessment in the 1930s and all but disappeared from the scene within fifteen years. If you don't know who your customers are, or how valuable they are to you, reread this book and follow Tom Peters' advice: Get close to your customer.

Another important trend is the rise of the employee. We are already seeing a shortage of qualified players in the 1990s, and as the world becomes more complex, the need for managerial and technological expertise will become ever greater. Unfortunately, our educational system is becoming less and less able to produce such expertise, which creates an ever-diminishing supply of people who are good at what they do. The obvious result will be that competent players will receive greatly increased respect and compensation and be given ever greater latitude to meet the needs of the customer. As Robert J. Ringer points out in his book *How to Find Happiness During the Collapse of Western Civilization*, such simple, obvious qualities as competence, integrity, and a willingness to work will put any player far ahead of the rest of the pack.

The rise of the employee will create a third trend, that of managers becoming facilitators of the great marriage of empowered players and valued consumers. No longer will managers be in place to direct the work; their job will be to free up employees to fully meet the needs of the customer.

Managers will be required to find better answers by a newly emancipated work force. Old practices of intimidation and harassment will no longer be tolerated. We may even see new ideas about who is working for whom. Such changes will send managers and leaders scrambling for new ideas, and the best answers will be found in the proven, time-honored, and obvious truths of the ages that have been overlooked for so long. We will seek role models in the biographies of great leaders and in such classics as *The Art of War*, by Sun Tzu. We will find new ideas and techniques by looking in other disciplines or arenas.

I was fascinated to listen to one of our creative executives in 1991 explain how he had used the "studio atmosphere" to create a corporate culture in his electronic game cartridge business. He spoke of company-wide retreats, offices without walls, and a collection of more than ten thousand Nerf balls that could be squeezed to release tension but, more important, were available for the periodic "Nerf alert," an updated version of the pillow fight. And I was even more impressed to learn that similar techniques were present in the development of the Walt Disney dynasty more than fifty years ago.

The new, worldwide quest for democracy in the marketplace will be matched by an increased voice of the people in the affairs of their governments. We will see taxpayer revolts, but revolts that will improve educational and social services. We will see new technological and ecological developments that will preserve the earth, reduce our dependence on fossil fuels, and help relieve hunger and poverty around the world.

Financially, we will realize that interest earned is better than interest paid. Consumers will reduce their level of debt and the interest associated with it and finally embrace the concept that the best interest earned is that not paid on discretionary purchases.

In fashion, value and durability will become more important than the fad of the moment. Consumers will demand the best but will continue to shop for it in factory outlets and mail-order houses where they will receive the greatest value for their money. These empowered consumers will ask for more value in interest rates, automobiles, and housing purchases and will wring greater value out of manufacturers and builders. We will become more animated on social issues and increasingly confused by the role of federal government in providing services. I hope the future will give us a return to the sanity of a balanced budget at the federal level and more citizen statesmen and stateswomen who will serve for the good of their constituents and not for the personal aggrandizement of the office. We will see increased concern about the quality of life and a desire for more recreation, reflection, and free time. We will continue to see a proliferation of ever more specialized goods and services for which people are willing to pay.

The future will continue to deepen and refine the trends of the present, keeping the things that work and rejecting the others, whether with the employees of an organization, the consumers of a product or service, or the people of a government. We will continue to discard what doesn't work and to borrow the things that are working elsewhere. In short, we will continue to improve. Continuous improvement is a permanent concept. It was in play long before Darwin and will survive long after Deming. It is our nature. It is our purpose. It is our only viable alternative.

For good or for bad, the future is coming. So we have to keep asking ourselves such questions as, "What are we doing that will no longer work three years from now?" "What do we need to learn?" "What do we need to ask our customers?" "What are we borrowing from other fields, from other businesses, from other technologies?" In short, the obvious thing we have to keep asking ourselves about the future is, "What are we doing about it—today?"

APPENDIX

I have referred to an asymptotic graph, scorecard, or analysis in several sections of this book. Let's expand on the concept and its various uses.

As a marketing major in college, I was not even aware that the shape of the 80/20 principle was called an asymptote. This is not a slam on the Michigan State University curriculum; it's just that the business students were not allowed to fraternize with the engineers. A client was kind enough to point it out in 1986, and I have tried to be scientifically correct since.

Its primary use is diagnostic. That helps sort the high payoff activities out of a large amount of data. For example, an insurance agent could use it reviewing his or her contract size or profitability. If you list the transactions in descending order, the largest "payoff" activity immediately floats to the top. The next step is the "obvious" discovery technique. Ask yourself:

- What is similar about these events?
- What behavior did I demonstrate to achieve these results?
- What causes can I reliably repeat to achieve similar results?

Often it is critical to view the same set of data or events through several screens. In the insurance example, it may not be enough to view it through the "total commissions" window. It may also be valuable to look at the contracts through the "contacts and/or appointments per contract" view. Another version may be the "dollars of commission/contract."

Another diagnostic view is that of a coach or supervisor for comparing the performance of several stores, locations, or individuals. **Do not, I repeat, do not use these scorecards for public display or comparison.** Their major benefit is the sorting out of patterns and results/behavior indicators. Use of these "forced rankings" is usually perceived as negative by players who have not chosen to compete on this comparative basis.

As a coaching tool, the enclosed example allowed our district manager to identify those stores that showed the greatest measure of improvement in average sale per customer in successive periods. It further allowed the coach to deliver kudos to the biggest winners, collect their experience, and pass it along to the less successful participants for their increased success next time. Without the utilization of the descending order diagnostic, the pattern of improvement was not obvious and therefore not recognizable or transmittable to other members of the team.

I believe the most important aspect of asymptotes is that they are natural—in that all groups of events, stores, or performers will naturally reflect these differences. We will not ever get the majority of results to exist within narrow upper and lower limits. There is a pattern of excellence emerging from the masses of data, people, and opportunities. The value of the format of analysis is that it expands the ease of recognizing the obvious.

Sample—How to Do Accumulated Averages
(Proper sequence of lines on a scoreboard)

"WIDGITS" PRODUCED

Column 1   Date

Column 2   Number of days since the beginning of the report period.

Column 3   Number of widgits produced on that date.

Column 4   Total number of widgits produced since the report period began. This number is the total of all the figures in column 3 up to the date you are entering the data.

Column 5   Take the number you have just entered in column 4 for today and divide it by the number in column 2. This is the basis for your "track record" of how many widgits you would have produced on an average day.

Column 6   Add the accumulated widgits for the past 5 days, including today. So, for day 6, you would add the figures in column 3 for days 2 through 6; and for day 18, you would add the figures in column 3 for days 14 through 18.

Column 7   To get this figure, take the number entered in column 6 for today and divide this by 5. This figure tells you your average production rate within the past 5 days. You will want to compare this with column 5 to see if your trend in production is improving over your average production rate.

SAMPLE—HOW TO DO ACCUMULATED AVERAGES
WIDGITS PRODUCED

COLUMN 1	COLUMN 2	ACTUAL COLUMN 3	COLUMN 4	MEAN COLUMN 5	COLUMN 6	ROLLING COLUMN 7
DATE	DAY	# WIDGITS	ACCUM. # WIDGITS	AVG. WIDGITS PER DAY	ACCUM. WIDGITS PAST 5 DAYS	AVG. G. WIDGITS PAST 5 DAYS
4/1	1	31	31	31		N/A
4/2	2	19	50	25		N/A
4/3	3	48	98	32.7		N/A
4/4	4	44	142	35.5		N/A
4/5	5	45	187	37.4	187	37.4
4/6	6	41	228	38	197	39.4
4/7	7	32	260	37.1	210	42
4/8	8	39	299	37.4	201	40.2
4/9	9	57	356	39.5	214	42.8
4/10	10	47	403	40.3	216	43.2
4/11	11	47	450	40.9	222	44.4
4/12	12	41	491	40.9	231	46.2
4/13	13	43	534	41.1	235	47
4/14	14	39	573	40.9	217	43.4
4/15	15	48	621	41.4	218	43.6
4/16	16	52	673	42.1	223	44.6
4/17	17	41	714	42	223	44.6
4/18	18	22	736	40.9	202	40.4
4/19	19	57	793	41.7	220	44
4/20	20	51	844	42.2	223	44.6

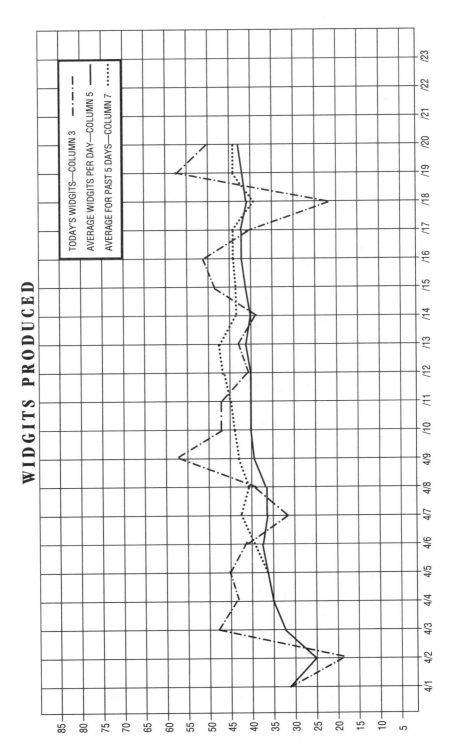

SAMPLE—MEAN_____ **BETWEEN**_____

VOLUME

Column 1   Sales numbered consecutively, beginning with 1.

Column 2   Date of sale

CAREER

Column 3   Number of days since last sale.

Column 4   Accumulative total of column 3.

Column 5   Running average of days between sales (column 4 divided by column 1).

LAST 5 SALES

Column 6   Total of days between sales for the past 5 sales.

Column 7   Average days between sales for the last five sales (column 6 divided by column 5). Always divide by 5, not by column 5.

DOLLARS PER SALE

Column 8   Amount of dollars per sale (sales volume or commissions earned).

Column 9   Accumulative total of column 8.

Column 10   Average sales volume or commissions per sale (column 9 divided by column 1).

Column 11   Total dollar value or commission earned on the past 5 sales.

Column 12   Average of dollars per sale or commission for the past 5 sales (column 12 divided by 5).

The purpose of this graph is to give you a clear idea of how your day-to-day sales are improving or decreasing in volume and dollars per sale.

It will give you an individual sale reading and also a running average that will show you an overall view of your sales proficiency. A five-sale average is included that gives a more current average.

SAMPLE—MEAN ——— BETWEEN ———

			VOLUME				DOLLARS PER SALE				
COLUMN 1	COLUMN 2	COLUMN 3	COLUMN 4	COLUMN 5	COLUMN 6	COLUMN 7	COLUMN 8	COLUMN 9	COLUMN 10	COLUMN 11	COLUMN 12
					****MEAN DAYS BETWEEN SALES CAREER / FIVE SALES						
SALE NUMBER	DATE	# DAYS	ACCUM.	MDBS	ACCUM.	MDBS	$/SALE	ACCUM. SALES $	AVERAGE SALE	TOTAL PAST 5 SALES	AVERAGE PAST 5 SALES
1	22-FEB-91	6	6	6.00			$1,500	$1,500	$1,500		
2	26-FEB-91	3	9	4.50			800	2,300	1,150		
3	12-MAR-91	10	19	6.33			500	2,800,	933		
4	19-APR-91	27	46	11.50			750	3,550	888		
5	20-MAY-91	22	68	13.60	68	13.6	500	4,050	810	$4,050	$810
6	22-MAY-91	1	69	11.50	63	12.6	250	4,300	717	2,800	560
7	28-MAY-91	4	73	10.43	64	12.8	900	5,200	743	2,900	580
8	20-JUN-91	16	89	11.13	70	14.0	1,000	6,200	775	3,400	680
9	26-JUN-91	4	93	10.33	47	9.4	200	6,400	711	2,850	570
10	15-JUL-91	14	107	10.70	39	7.8	600	7,000	700	2,950	590
11	15-AUG-91	22	129	11.73	60	12.0	750	7,750	705	3,450	690
12	10-SEP-91	19	148	12.33	75	15.0	800	8,550	713	3,350	670
13	01-OCT-91	15	163	12.54	74	14.8	1,000	9,550	735	3,350	670

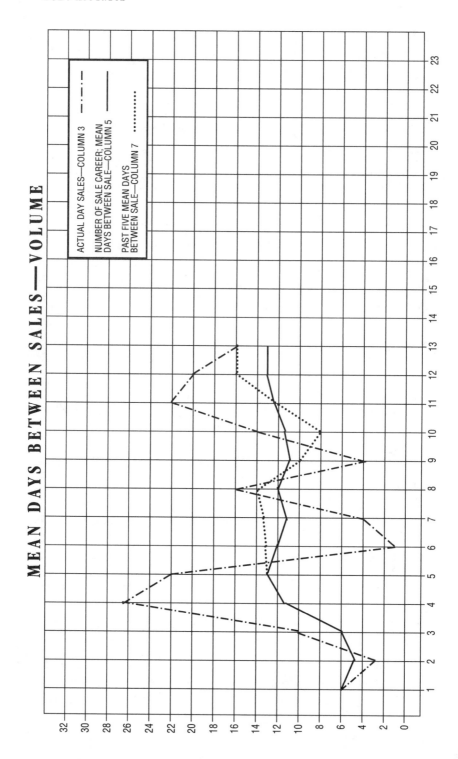

MEAN DAYS BETWEEN SALES—VOLUME

ACTUAL DAY SALES—COLUMN 3

NUMBER OF SALE CAREER: MEAN
DAYS BETWEEN SALE—COLUMN 5

PAST FIVE MEAN DAYS
BETWEEN SALE—COLUMN 7

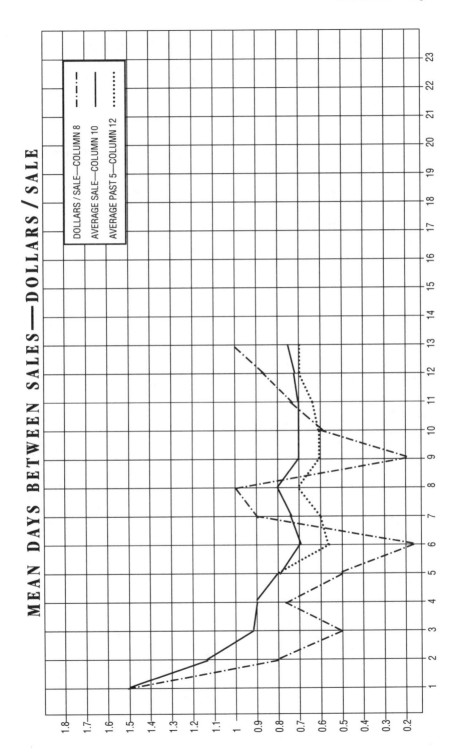

RESULTS TO RESOURCES RATIO
EXAMPLE: IDENTIFYING RESULTS

List the Results

The major results for which the person or team is responsible are listed. These should be the principle reasons for which the position exists. Of course, the results measured should be limited to those over which the person has control. We have listed the possible results for our sample hotel below.

*Specific Results	Resources
Rooms rented	
Room rate	
Advanced bookings	
Repeat / return reservations	
Gross income	
Net income	
Customer satisfaction	
Conventions booked	
Restaurant sales	
Convention income	
Banquets booked	
Banquet / convention income	
Cash flow (outstanding accounts, deposits, etc.)	

Note: These are managerial results. Rooms cleaned, invoices on time, reservations without error, on-time airport pickups, and hundreds of other scorekeeping opportunities are also to be developed for all teams or individuals.

RESULTS TO RESOURCES RATIO
EXAMPLE: IDENTIFYING RESOURCES

LIST THE RESOURCES

The major resources or opportunities available to produce the results are listed. These are measurable elements from resource categories such as time, facility, space, people, equipment, materials, money, etc.

*Specific Results	Resources
	Time
	Days
	Weeks
	Months
	Years
	Paid labor hours
	Square footage of convention space
	Total number of rooms
	Rooms rented each night
	Total guests in hotel
	Capital invested
	Marketing
	Leads generated
	Contacts called
	Ads run
	Mailers mailed
	Community activities scheduled/held
	Budget $
	Total convention $ in town
	Total conference rooms rented in town or area
	Total inquiries or calls for info
	Total number of guests

RESULTS TO RESOURCES RATIO EXAMPLE: MATCH THE RESULTS TO THE RESOURCES

PRIORITIZE THE RESOURCES AND THE RESULTS

*Specific Results	Resources
Rooms rented	Time
Room rate	Days
Advanced bookings	Weeks
Repeat / return reservations	Months
Gross income	Years
Net income	Paid labor hours
Customer satisfaction	Square footage of convention space
Conventions booked	Total number of rooms
Restaurant sales	Rooms rented each night
Convention income	Total guests in hotel
Banquets booked	Capital invested
Banquet / convention income	Marketing
Cash flow (outstanding	Leads generated
accounts, deposits, etc.)	Contacts called
	Ads run
	Mailers mailed
	Community activities scheduled/held
	Budget $
	Total convention $ in town
	Total conference rooms rented in town or area
	Total inquiries or calls for info
	Total number of guests

Rank the first few results and match the most significant resources to go with them.

PROVIDES RESULTS TO RESOURCES RATIOS LIKE THESE:

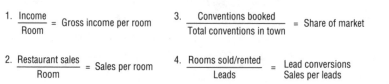

1. $\dfrac{\text{Income}}{\text{Room}}$ = Gross income per room

2. $\dfrac{\text{Restaurant sales}}{\text{Room}}$ = Sales per room

3. $\dfrac{\text{Conventions booked}}{\text{Total conventions in town}}$ = Share of market

4. $\dfrac{\text{Rooms sold/rented}}{\text{Leads}}$ = Lead conversions / Sales per leads

RESULTS TO RESOURCES RATIO
PERSONAL OR TEAM RESULTS
TO RESOURCES RATIO

One output or result of this team / unit / job is:

_____

Step II: List Results	Step I: List Resources

Step 3: Prioritize resources	Steps 7-8-9: Draw a relationship
Step 4: Prioritize results	between important resources and
Step 5: Enumerate / Digitize resources	important results to create three
Step 6: Enumerate / Digitize results	primary RRR's.

INDEX

If you like the ideas in this book and are interested in learning more about the services offered by **The Game of Work**, please call 1-800-438-6074.

Companies and associations internationally depend on the author of *The Game of Work* and *Managing the Obvious* to motivate and inspire them to new levels of success, both on and off the job. With his help, you can count on an improved bottom line, with increased employee enthusiasm and productivity.

Find out what Pepsi-Cola, Fleming Companies Inc., Dow Chemical, First Interstate Bank, American Stores, General Foods Corporation, International Paper, Browning Ferris Industries, and thousands of other industry leaders know about the proven principles we teach and our guaranteed results.